Spectral Realms

No. 13 ‡ Summer 2020

Edited by S. T. Joshi

The spectral realms that thou canst see
With eyes veil'd from the world and me.

H. P. LOVECRAFT, "To a Dreamer"

SPECTRAL REALMS is published twice a year by Hippocampus Press,
P.O. Box 641, New York, NY 10156 (www.hippocampuspress.com).
Copyright © 2020 by Hippocampus Press.
All works are copyright © 2020 by their respective authors.
Cover art and design by Daniel V. Sauer, dansauerdesign.com
Hippocampus Press logo by Anastasia Damianakos.

ISBN 978-1-61498-306-4   ISSN 2333-4215

Contents

Poems 5
  King Pest / Richard L. Tierney 7
  The Protector / Ian Futter 8
  After Verdun: A Psychomantic Vision / Manuel Pérez-Campos 11
  Märchen (Fairy Tales) / Carl E. Reed 12
  Nevermore / Adele Gardner 14
  The Sleeper / Josh Maybrook 15
  City of Skulls / Maxwell I. Gold 16
  Among the Petroglyphs / Ann K. Schwader 18
  The Catacombs / Tatiana Strange 19
  Illusion of Light / Ronald Terry 20
  The Hidebehind: A Legend of the North Country / Frank Coffman .. 22
  Dream Snatchers / Ngo Binh Anh Khoa 25
  My Bantam Black Fay / Manuel Arenas 26
  Doubled Word / Rahul Gupta 27
  De Quincey Mutations: Our Ladies of Sorrow / Wade German 30
  Ithaca, Finally / Darrell Schweitzer 33
  All That I Have Lost / Christina Sng 34
  Astray / F. J. Bergmann 38
  Imperishable / David C. Kopaska-Merkel 39
  Wraith of the Versifier / David Barker 40
  The Tongueless Dead / Leigh Blackmore 41
  Sanctuary / Mary Krawczak Wilson 42
  O Iranon / Charles Lovecraft 43
  Sweet Discordia Lee / Oliver Smith 44
  The Harvester / K. A. Opperman 47
  The Song of Calamity Joe / Andrey Pissantchev 48
  Jenkin / Ross Balcom 53
  Amongst the Sargasso / Scott J. Couturier 54
  Notre Dame Is Burning! / Lori R. Lopez 56
  The Sweet Dreams of the Dead / James O'Melia 61
  The Witch-Gallows / Josh Maybrook 62
  Lord Death / Ashley Dioses 63
  Our Lady of the Acherontia / Allan Rozinski 64

Legion / Benjamin Blake 67
Where the New Gods Dwell / Maxwell I. Gold 68
Imaginary Friend / Ngo Binh Anh Khoa... 70
Lines on Austin Osman Spare's "Arbor Vitae" / Manuel Pérez-
    Campos 75
In the Forest, Where Wild Things Live / Claire Smith 76
Melinoë / Wade German 78
Hell-Flower / Manuel Arenas 79
Haunted / Ronald Terry.. 80
He Who Waits / Frank Coffman... 81
Splenetic IV: After Baudelaire / Rahul Gupta 82
The Graves / Steven Withrow... 84
A Conspiracy Penetrated / Carl E. Reed 86
Frozen Voices / Leigh Blackmore... 87
Calling All Witches / Adele Gardner 88
To the Wolves / Scott J. Couturier 90
Red Land, Black Pharaoh / Ann K. Schwader 91
Ouroboros / Frank Coffman.. 92
The Draining Chair / Thomas Tyrrell.. 94
Retrieval / F. J. Bergmann 99
The Rider of the Pegasi / C. d. G. Nightingale 100
Testament of Doom: A Paean to Clark Ashton Smith / Manuel
    Pérez-Campos 102
The Passive Vampire / Wade German.. 103
The Pores of Earth / Charles Lovecraft 104
Moribond / Manuel Arenas 105
The Variant / Maxwell I. Gold.. 106
To Gaelle Lacroix, Lone Survivor of the Trufort Massacre /
    Steven Withrow 108
Dr. Ripper, I Presume? / Carl E. Reed... 111
Red Tresses / Scott C. Couturier 112

Classic Reprints... 113
  Strife / R. H. Barlow 115
  It Will Be Thus / Arthur Goodenough 116

Reviews 119
    The Sun Sings Loud and Clear / Donald Sidney-Fryer 121
    Terror and Poignancy / S. T. Joshi 130
    A Queen of Dark Poetry / Sunni K Brock 132
Notes on Contributors 134

Poems

King Pest

Richard L. Tierney

King Pest, his dread corona glittering on
His pallid skull, glides forth to blight the lands,
Clutching his gleaming scythe in bony hands,
A crimson harvest he shall reap anon!

His shadow falls across the shuddering world
As humans hide in fearful isolation,
Sensing his hollow laugh's reverberation
As o'er this cringing earth his curse is hurled.

The Protector

Ian Futter

I'd burn and break
the world of men
and then I'd do it
all again.
I'd stop strange planets
in their path
to see him smile
or hear him laugh.
I'd smother stars
just on a whim,
to spend a moment more
with him.
And if he walked
In valleys dark,
I'd stalk the beasts
that spied his spark,
and all dread demons
circling round,
I'd break their necks
and bring them down.

And if he's lost
amongst the trees
of grasping forests,
I would seize

his hand
and wrench him
from the sprites
Who'd hold him
in their endless night.

And should he slip
to caverns deep
and bring Belial
back from his sleep,
I'd walk into the stifling gloom
and send the Behemoth
to his doom.

And pedlar trolls,
with all their wares,
who brought my friend
so many cares
beneath their bridges,
I would catch
to cut their throats
and them dispatch.

And every time
his footsteps strayed,
I'd warn the monsters

that he'd made
to keep their distance—
every one—
Until his feet
should find the sun.

After Verdun: A Psychomantic Vision

Manuel Pérez-Campos

No more screams for bayonets amid snap of sanity
by trench-heating flash or breaches caused by blind
commands ignored in terror. Cartilaginous, white-stringed
scarecrows with shredded faces lie entousled in haggard,
belated indignation, clenching still with charred, stripped
knuckles a quantum of that barb-wired, tree-stumped mud
tract in a trauma-brokered blitz of tightened breath and
pulse in which now bloom shattered teeth and bullet-
scarred helmets. Unable to dispel excesses perpetrated,
their spectres, those crazed, streamer-like things emanated
upward by land mine-reaped mounds of uniform-bursting
flesh, join hands, forced by darkling angels, and twirl with
gathering momentum until an opaquely populated twister
in the astral plane over the poison gas stench that even now
pervades this blanked-out realm and in which all howl,
nauseated, to left and right because each other's hell-spawn.

Märchen (Fairy Tales)

Carl E. Reed

Magda recites the ancient *fabeln*
    savage, dark, & grim:
wolves & witches, lost little boys,
    kobolds, trolls—"Again!"

Wide-eyed Günter demands of *mutter*
    entranced by her cadenced words;
fire crackling in field-stoned *flett*
    the cattle lowing, a weird

counterpoint to alto utterance
    in that shadowed, smoky *einhaus*—
the pungent scent of new-mown hay
    a whisper-squeak of *grau maus*.

Outside: the rising howl of wind
    A flash! A rolling boom!
Thor unleashing lightning & thunder
    inside, in warmth & gloom.

Günter hangs on every word
    bewitching *mutter* chants;
his scalp hair prickles; he pants in fear—
    Ghouls! Ghosts! Vampires! Plants:

nightshade, hemlock, stinging nettle
    towering holy oak;
lambent flame & groaning stone
    oily corpse-black smoke.

The tales are void of sentiment
    they are hard, unflinching, medieval;
& Günter knows a shivery thrill
    of terror quite primeval.

Scheming warlocks, moaning spectres
    fiends miniscule & fey;
berserker giants, monstrous *vaters*,
    beasts that stalk & slay.

Magda recites the ancient *fabeln*
    savage, dark, & grim:
wolves & witches, lost little boys,
    kobolds, trolls—"Again!"

Nevermore

Adele Gardner

No one now living knows the truth—
Edgar, your mysterious death haunts me
Vigorously, as relentless as Montresor
Entombing his former friend.
Revenge for your Raven or your many loves?
Murder as vile as your tales, your character assassinated
Only too well by Griswold—vile as your worst villains.
Ravens roost on your grave, carrying messages to
Everyone you ever loved.

The Sleeper

Josh Maybrook

Immersed in dreams dread Cthulhu lies
Amid his city's sunken heap,
A marvel fallen to demise
Beneath the starless deep.

A fallen god, he never dies
But waits alone in restless sleep
Until the day that he shall rise
From out the frigid deep.

City of Skulls

Maxwell I. Gold

Inside the emptiness of my dreams, towering palaces of marble, stone, and jade crumbled over the inexorable aeons, wishing for swift ruin. The streets were filled with cracked skulls, whose ripped crania spilled liquid nightmares onto the pavement of the dream-city. Crackling tones pierced my ears as I stepped over the brittle pieces of ivory and decayed calcite, their sorrowful tears pouring into the rusted sewers. I dared not imagine the terror that ravaged this city or wonder at its true primal nature.

Toward the broken horizon, underneath silver stars where calamitous galaxies swirled in oceans of oblivion, I felt bathed in their tears of falling stardust. The tears that were shed for a city whose ideas were now preserved in plastic stood as a remnant of that silicone society. I treaded further, into the bleak alleyways, alongside cold towers whose insides were torn apart. A soulless wind scratched against their frames, its cold chill throttling my scream. It was then I knew something sinister had permeated the space within my dreams—a viral darkness so ancient that its apotheosis was likened to that which soaked the nameless city in evil.

I began to run faster, feeling each step crunching on the littered streets. My nerves rattled as bile thickened, darkened, poured from the eyes of those broken skulls. Something was coming, anxiously waiting to consume me. The wind howled again as I reached the edges of the crumbling city, obstinately protesting its doom. The skies began to ooze a disfigured coloration of gold, diamonds, and radioactive particulates that formed a dismal yellow burst of light.

As I fell to my knees, a piercing tone ruptured my insides, with a pain in my head following as black bile dripped from my ears. The misty haze of the timeless day soon filled my eyes. As the heavy scent of rust and blood congested my pores, it was then that I realized I stood before that Nuclear God, whereupon at the bottom of the universe it sat on a throne built from the bones of a thousand dead races, waiting with a dark entropic sanguinity.

A corrosive paresthesia soon overtook my body as I slammed into the pavement. There was nothing more, nothing left as the scent of miasmal sludge slowly filled my every orifice. The muted tones of gold and brown painted my weary eyelids shut, with a heavy palette of spectral discoloration.

Lost inside the emptiness of my dreams, towering palaces of marble, stone, and jade crumbled over the inexorable aeons and the streets were filled with my cracked skulls.

Among the Petroglyphs

Ann K. Schwader

The archaeologist who led us claimed
no meaning for this muttering of lines
incised in desert varnish. Vague designs
like mutant constellations—serpents maimed
to broken lightning—beasts turned fever dreams
invading daylight—none of them were more
or less than mysteries. Yet long before
their makers tasted breath, our cosmos teemed
with just such myths made flesh. With just such gods
as nightmares name in whispers . . . or in texts
that left me shaken, pallid & perplexed
past sanity. Abandoning the broad
& common trail, I scrambled up alone
in answer to some dreadful summons. There
a terror I shall carry to my grave
awaited me: within one narrow cave,
a hundred graven pipers filled the air
with praise to Azathoth from voids unknown.

The Catacombs

Tatiana Strange

I found myself in the catacombs far beneath the streets;
As I wandered deeper into those dark passages civilization faded
    completely.
The city above is unaware of the kingdom of dead beneath their feet;
There the dead lay in piles of dusty bones collected over time,
Lost, forgotten, and cloaked in misery as the poor souls had been in life,
A sparkling metropolis built upon the ruins of their demise.

The lonesome skulls look to me wistfully through the darkness of hollow
    eyes;
Shadows flicker, then faint moaning I hear,
Oh, such tragic songs the dead sing . . .
Thousands of bones strewn about like the pieces of a broken mirror,
A reflection of Death or only the remnants of what Death brings?
In these catacombs the dead lay with all their broken dreams:
Is this how they envisioned their eternal peace?

A mass grave for the undesired and the broken,
I found no dark adventure there, no timeless mystery,
Merely Death's twisted orchestra, its tragedy silent and unspoken.
I return to the world above before the dead cling to me,
Leaving the empire of bones far below,
In the macabre sombreness of the catacombs.

Illusion of Light

Ronald Terry

I am not descended from my father.
One night a homeless ghost
looked through the window;
Its longing became me,
and I became its forgotten child.

One light still burns in the house;
All the others have gone dark.
A shadow sits by my side,
lodged in my left eye.
It looks like me
but is something else.

Only when I was young
was I really myself.
Under cold blue flames
I'm left an old man with cold hands,
a ghost in my own house.

The mind sinks into its own thought,
drifting through tunnels
that never open into the sun.

But upon illumination
of god's eternal statue,
come into the light.
Let me see
what is real
and what is not.

The Hidebehind: A Legend of the North Country

(a poem in Split Couplets)

Frank Coffman

Our Forests teem with things to fear—
And some come near.

Of course the wolf and Grizzly Bear
Can be found there.

And cougars to West and angered moose
In East are loose.

But there are some, to most unknown—
From a different zone.

A thing that lives in Northern Wood
Takes folk for food!

The legend warns all those who stray
Past light of day.

The tales all tell a ferocious beast
Will have a feast.

For human flesh—its favorite food!
It craves man's blood!

It is well known some lumbermen
Don't return again.

And yet no one can tell its shape,
For few escape.

The thing will hide behind a tree
So none can see.

Concealed by boulder it will lurk—
Then do its work!

Some say—who've lived—a sense of Fear
Grows when it's near.

But all insist it has a knack
To be in back!

Intestines are its favorite part!
Sometimes the heart!

And all too oft remains are found
Upon cold ground.

So nights—though not logging—lumberjacks
Carry their axe.

But most, by the warm fire of the stove,
Refuse to rove.

Far better to be wary and not find
The Hidebehind.

Dream Snatchers

Ngo Binh Anh Khoa

From what foul Pit they sprang, I cannot tell,
But in my dreams I'd see those leathery wings
That lift the skeletal frames of faceless things
With fangs drenched in the purplish flames of Hell.
The horde came, blackening my mindscape's sky,
Till what remained was shadow, deep and dark,
And like a fiendish choir, they'd madly bark;
Harsh growls and piercing shrieks rang far and nigh.
One, without warning, bit into my flesh
And grabbed me, heedless of the cries I'd make;
Then, on a bone-erected Nest, I'd wake,
Where swarmed starved maggots yearning for food fresh.
How long have I been trapped here? I know naught
As I, in endless waking nightmares, rot.

My Bantam Black Fay

Manuel Arenas

I have a little manikin that sleeps inside a cask;
I feed him blood from my left hand then he does what I ask.
He follows me wheree'r I go, perdu to all but me;
Occulted from the Christian eye thro' impish sorcery.
Conflagrant eyes sear, mesmerize with their perfervid glance.
His silver tongue glints as he speaks to cinch me in a trance.
He whispers secrets in my ear, to make one's hair turn white,
Then whisks me off on leathern wings to join a black mass rite.
He'll raze your home and salt your fields, he'll even taint your well;
He'll change your children out for sidhe, then drag your soul to Hell.
He's my infernal instructor, a boon from the Dark Lord;
And when I'm burning at the stake he's sworn misericorde.
His name is unpronounceable for human tongues to say,
So I just call him by the name of My Bantam Black Fay.

Doubled Word

Rahul Gupta

> There was a man of double deed,
> Who sowed his garden full of seed;
> When the seed began to grow,
> 'Twas like a garden full of snow ...
>
> —Anon., traditional nursery rhyme

There was born of troubled breed
An infant who would always feed,
Yet in his crib would scarcely show
He'd ever find the strength to grow:
For, as they couldn't know, his cries
Were caterpillars in his eyes
Like worms that gnawed at him in bed
Or serpents crawling in his head,
Knotting there the tangled skein
That formed the windings of his brain,
And from whose fangs the venom streams
To light the furnace of his dreams.
Then was a man, of troubled need,
Who trod a map he could not read;
When the map became a maze,
'Twas like his labyrinth of days;
When pacing every twist and turn,
'Twas then he found he was alone;
The panorama of his grief
Perplexed his heart beyond relief.

When he saw his own mistake,
'Twas then his heart began to break;
When the tears of his despair
Froze to ice amid thin air,
'Twas like a cell with walls of glass
He could not tell how to bypass,
Which mirrored, not him, but instead
The nightmare-faces of the dead.
To hear the music of the ice
Thawing, he'd thought would suffice,
But when the walls began to melt,
'Twas like delight could not be felt;
When every nerve began to dull,
'Twas like the spider in his skull
Laying there her clutch of eggs
With every shudder of her legs;
When he tried to utter word
'Twas like he never could be heard
Because the teeming hive had flung
Their filaments across his tongue;
When his tongue began to shrink
'Twas then he found he could not think,
For no matter how he'd fought

They'd gobbled up his every thought.
Now when he doddered hobble-kneed,
'Twas like his life began to bleed
Away, as though to him decreed
No health, no wealth: but Death indeed.

De Quincey Mutations: Our Ladies of Sorrow

Wade German

"Three sisters they are, of one mysterious household; and their paths are wide apart; but of their dominion there is no end."
—Thomas De Quincey, *Suspiria de Profundis*

I. Mater Lachrymarum

All night and day, her phantom raves and moans
For vanished faces, innocents interred;
Her eerie lamentations can be heard
Across the sky from outer darks unknown.

Madonna fed on pain, she discreates
All peace for those who sob with litanies.
Upon her girdle hang the many keys
Which open every dwelling's doors or gates:

By power of those keys, and like a ghost,
She glides into the homes of mourning souls
Who sleepless in their grief, would surely sleep;

But gather to her bosom, as one host,
And raise the requiem which ever rolls
Through chambers of her mausolean keep.

II. Mater Suspiriorum

She raises not her eyes with hope to find
The star of mercy risen to redeem;
Her downcast gaze holds only perished dreams,
Immersed in murky fathoms of her mind.

She harbours wrecks of untold lives unwrought,
But never weeps—perpetually she sighs;
She clamours not, nor misery defies,
Her aspect humble, abject, undistraught.

If she may murmur, it is in her sleep;
Whisper she may, but to herself at night.
Mutter she does, on desolate black shores,

In ruins sunk in solitary deeps,
Where one might meet her, keeping to her rite,
And hear her verses of sepulchral lore.

III. Mater Tenebrarum

One whispers while we dare to talk of *her!*
Her kingdom has one law: no flesh should live.
Mother of lunacies, her gift to give:
Suggesting suicide the soul makes pure.

Her eyes shine darkling lights defying God,
Illuminations blacker than the void.
In her dominion, all who are destroyed
Shall rise again from out unhallowed sod:

Received in her embrace as by a hearse,
Each is anointed and absolved of past,
Then banished to black chapels beyond hope:

Abominated by her kiss and curse,
They enter elder truths, vile truths at last,
Beneath her mouldy earth as worms that grope.

Ithaca, Finally

Darrell Schweitzer

Yes, the voyage was long.
Yes, he visited exotic ports,
Egyptian cities, Phoenician markets.
Yes, he acquired rare goods
and sat at the feet of sages.
Many were the summer sunrises,
many the winter evenings,
with a bit of piracy and rape on the side,
to keep the crew occupied.
He defied the Laestrygonians and the Cyclops;
He did not fear the wrath of Poseidon,
though he clearly should have,
and in the end he lost it all,
treasures dumped into the sea, ships sunk,
every last one of his faithful, greedy sailors
dead, wailing at him in the underworld.
When he got home at last, what did he,
a ragged an wretched wanderer
bring as a gift?
He made his son a murderer;
He spread desolation most generously.
He would have started another war
had not Zeus intervened.
In his return, there was no happiness.
Better that the voyage had never ended.

All That I Have Lost

Christina Sng

I've been lost for years now,
Trapped in one skin or another,
Living the lives of strangers,
Eating the fare of others.

All I remember for certain
Is I crawled out of my grave
One blinding summer afternoon
To the shocked face of a girl,

Picking up her football
From a nearby mulberry bush.
My bloodied hands ached
For the longest of days

Till I found my way
To an abandoned hut
Hidden in a hedge maze
On a haunted property

In the middle of nowhere,
Living off the land,
Eating squirrel and rabbit
Caught with my own hands.

Who am I, I wondered
For a life and an age.

After a time I stopped
Wondering and just lived.

Then they found me,
These people, my family.
There was elation sparking
In my tired, addled brain.

The scent of the children
Brought a comforting joy;
But less so the man
Supposedly my mate.

I followed them home
To an unfamiliar place;
I recognized nothing
But my children's sweet gaze.

That night I slept beside them,
Holding them tight.
I woke up an hour later
To a full-blown panic attack.

Quietly I treaded barefoot
Across the tiny room,
Reached out to lock the door
And stayed awake till noon.

The next day while tidying,
I unearthed a loose floorboard.
Inside lay the torn pages
Of my long-forgotten thoughts.

There, I learned my story,
One of terror and fear,
One that ended with a shovel
Smashed into my ear.

He buried me shallow
At the back of the woods;
But something brought me back,
Something that could.

I carried the sleeping children
Into the idling family car,
Searched the garage
For a bottle of black tar,

Poured it relentlessly
Over his twisted, snoring face,
Watched his eyes pop out,
Turning crimson and crazed.

"Scream and wake the kids,"
I hissed, echoing his taunt.
The memories returned
In a bloody full force.

I left the house in flames,
Driving back to my hut.
There, the children and I
Lived safe and untouched,

Until inevitably,
They grew up and moved out.
Now I am lost again,
Wandering around in circles,

Wondering which life is real
And which is not.
The only real thing for certain
Is my shovel-shaped head notch,

And the children who visit,
Once wisps, now doves.

Astray

F. J. Bergmann

I am lost in the dark forest. But not alone.
If only I had realized the transformation,
known you had changed, recognized you
despite the spell . . . I can yet regret my impulse
to kill. I did not understand what you had become,
enchanted, did not know of the curse you were under,
did not know you loved me even so. When the wolf
leapt past me out the window, I called for hounds,
huntsmen, never missing you. I can claim I thought
to protect you, but you will not understand why
I did not cry out your name, search for you.
Why was the gold chain I had given you
still around the wolf's neck? Where are you?

Imperishable

David C. Kopaska-Merkel

Naked in your tomb,
no name legible above the door,
but your skin so smooth, unblemished,
your teeth long and sharp,
bones in a crumbling pile
against the wall
were never yours.

Imperishable Queen,
or King,
what does it matter
to the terrified ones
struggling in your iron embrace,
sucked dry
as old bones?

Wraith of the Versifier

David Barker

From tomb to tomb the ragged warlock sweeps,
Performing rites condemned by righteous men,
While in his wake a fierce familiar creeps,
Alert for all who would invade their ken.
Arriving at the poetess's stone,
Where many come to mourn her sad demise,
A necromantic song they soft intone,
In hopes her withered form might stir and rise.

And rise she does, her headstone tilts and falls.
The soil beneath erupts, a seething mass
Of coffin splinters, mixed with bone and gore—
Thrust up, an arm on which a grave worm crawls.
Her decayed lips emit a charnel gas,
Proclaiming she will utter rhymes no more.

The Tongueless Dead
(for Thomas Lovell Beddoes)

Leigh Blackmore

Bleak autumn falls upon the mossy graves,
Pale flesh falls from cadavers as if flayed.
Graverobbers there and other evil knaves
Dig up fresh corpses for the doctor's blade.

The foetid earth and roots yield to their spades.
Old, tongueless dead lie still, their skulls and bones
Abandoned by their long-gone fleshless shades.
Graverobbers care not; now they break the stones

That bar the way and keep them from their prize—
The fat, sleek dead new-buried in their tombs.
To carry off the dead they don disguise
That hides them from the watchmen in their rooms.

Dark Death will feast, a lasting requiem
For graveyard, morgue, and fatal hanging tree;
So amply feed the appetites of them
Who would make coin from human misery.

Sanctuary

Mary Krawczak Wilson

You were my sanctuary
When I was feeling wary
Of where the road would take me
In my quest to forage free.

You were my sanctuary
When we agreed to marry
And fuse our souls as one—
Bold and radiant sun.

You were my sanctuary
When we sought home on a prairie
Where keening winds were hell
And ripped our souls apart as well.

You were my sanctuary
When the North Star shone bright;
Now light and sky are leaden,
My love for you has deadened.

There is no sanctuary
When the beast in you is free
To capture me in its claws
And crush me with its jaws.

O Iranon

Charles Lovecraft

Bright Iranon, the gorgeous Aira waits
For your young step to wander cobbled ways,
With gleaming eyes bejewelled with shining haze
And in your beating breast a breath that bates.
O, you were never born for common states,
For you had found the far superior blaze
Of fair dream witcheries, with which to raze
And break the wretched thrall of life's grey gates.

The granite city of Teloth you crossed
With Romnod, and shared years of thoughtless pride,
But at the last you starkly went *inside*.
You stepped into the sands and found the cost,
    Not recognizing dream for what it was,
        A false and gaily painted albatross.

Sweet Discordia Lee

Oliver Smith

Sweet Discordia; a picture
on a crumbling yellowed page.
Her face as fair as a summer day:
in John Caryth a wildfire raged.
In his heart she lit a fever;
down the leaf-walled lanes he ran,
beyond the church, to a pretty grove
by the gentle babbling stream.
He thought that there lay Paradise,
by way of Witches' Green.

Above John, like a grinning skull,
in darkness glowed the moon.
And by the roots of the twisted yew,
among the ancient mossy graves,
John found the witch's tomb.
Bold her lichened statue stood:
her stone arms in triumph spread;
and on her head a stony hood;
and carved at her marble feet
her name, a thousand curses deep.

In his fever and in the fire
John prayed that her heart might beat;
that her emerald eyes might see;
that her ruby lips might open;

that again her tongue might speak;
that he might be her chosen
and might learn her heart to keep.
He offered her his blood and pain:
beside the dreadful doorway stone
three times John called her name;

three times he knocked as he sacrificed;
Three times he cursed and wailed.
Beneath the tower and timeless clock
John waited for the midnight chimes
and in the darkness watched.
When sudden at his side stood she:
her hand so cold, her face so pale:
the prettiest one, to him spoke she,
"For just one night I return again,
 I am dead Discordia Lee."

She led John through firefly-woods,
over brook and steep hillside;
to the witches' temple in the trees
in grassy glade where pale worms crawl,
and where the grave-born feed;
where owls and moths take flight
among the stars and over field;

In the graveyard where beetles nest
she plucked for John an alien flower
from the phosphorescent mist.

She laid beside John on the moss;
enchanted in the pale moonbeams
their beating hearts she crossed.
But in the morning like some dream
Sweet Discordia Lee he lost:
Now still her shadow whispers
and John's rambling tongue it cries,
for his heart is buried with her
and he must wait, until the end of time,
for Discordia Lee to rise.

The Harvester

K. A. Opperman

He comes from the cornfield at first fall of dark,
With rusty old sickle and russet red cloak,
To take what is left him and follow the spark
Of flickering pumpkins while night-ravens croak.

A gourd or a corncob is all he requires,
A nut-cup of acorns, an apple, some cakes,
But they who would take the town elders for liars,
Ignoring old legends, will rue their mistakes.

The Harvester takes what a household can give—
When crops go unoffered, a life will suffice.
On All Hallows' Even, if all are to live,
'Tis better to pay him his portion, his price.

If ever such figure should come to your door
With basket of wicker while kids trick-or-treat,
'Tis best to remember the stories of yore,
And fill up his basket with many a sweet.

The Song of Calamity Joe

Andrey Pissantchev

I sit in a bunker
Alone
When a nicotine cackle sounds in my ear:
"Why so glum, boy?" he asks, and I sigh.
I tell him of my post-apocalyptic sorrows
Of pain and ruin and loneliness.
Calamity Joe simply snickers again
Raining acrid spittle on my face.
"My boy," he says, "lad!
You're looking at this from the wrong side!"
He grabs hold of my arm—
Bony hook-fingers digging into my skin—
Tips his top hat jauntily and
Bursts into song:

> *Sure, the land is all toxic slush*
> *And all your pals have turned into mush*
> *And humanity's ruins to the west and the east*
> *Are swarming with ravenous flesh-eating beasts.*
>
> *But there's so much to this new world of ours,*
> *So much more than toxic rain showers,*
> *A whole new life of excitement and fun*
> *A blast of a time—if you'll pardon my pun.*

He cracks the vault door open,
Beckons me to follow.
I shrug and
I do.

*　*　*

We find ourselves at the top of a hill
Where the sunrise skies
Are clouded with green, black and purple.
Calamity Joe sweeps his arms with pathos.

> *In the old days, before everything broke,*
> *A city was here, filled with boring old folk.*
> *Nine-to-five doldrums, work shallow and vain,*
> *A sea of drab concrete. A visual stain!*
>
> *Now take a deep breath, boy, and look at this sight:*
> *These colours, these poisons, this beautiful blight.*
> *This landscape of ruins and molten debris*
> *Is a blank slate, a new start, almost for free!*

I breathe deep as he asked
And cough out blood.
And while flashes of lightning
Illuminate his unnatural grin

I do have to admit
The clouds do kind of look beautiful.

                    *   *   *

The afternoon we are at the stream,
Jumping from stone onto stone onto rusted car husk.
Calamity Joe sings his tune
And plastic-filled fish listen.

> *Adventure waits at every corner, boy,*
> *This barren waste brims full of joy;*
> *In this playground of wreckage, a graveyard haunt,*
> *You can be anything you want:*
>
> *You can be a hero, scavenger, a thug,*
> *You can trip all day on some acquired drug,*
> *You can do anything that pops into your head,*
> *There is no boss to tell you off and God is dead.*

I can almost see his point
As a child-sized skeleton floats past,
But I still can't meet his mad swivelling eyes.
"Not convinced, eh?" he chuckles.
"Come. I'll show you my favourite part."

* * *

We stalk the ghostly concrete rubble
Where three walls of a warehouse miraculously stand.
Calamity Joe speaks, *sotto voce*,
Backed by a whispered chorus of unnamed things
In the debris around us.

> *We are almost there, where my song ends;*
> *We're here to meet a lovely host of friends.*

> *What? Friends? What friends?* (I ask, not sold)

> (He laughs) *My friends. Your friends. Behold!*

He flips a switch
And the structure illuminates, revealing
A shifting mass of formless monsters.
I freeze and Calamity Joe waltzes in,
Pirouettes among them, singing:

> *You were lonely once, my fine old chum,*
> *You hid away, all down and numb.*
> *So lift your sadness, kick your pangs,*
> *Then lighten up and meet the gang!*

Heptapods with gleaming foot-wide eyes,
Half-bats half-sharks half-wolves half-flies,
Gibbering amalgamates of meat and bone
That reach out, snarl and melt and moan.

My world spins as the pungent stench
Of the beasts assaults me.
I see Calamity Joe wink and
Disappear.
"Where did you go?" I ask.
All the while tentacles tug at my limbs
And as my flesh gets appropriated by the huddle
I feel well, calm and welcome.
With my last vestige of individuality I think:
"You know what?
The end of the world isn't half-bad after all."

Jenkin

Ross Balcom

The firmament: stars and planets
Run like rats in their courses.

Brown Jenkin has eaten my face.
I must cancel my date with your daughter.

Arkham celebrates the Rodent Mass.
My tail, newly emerged, twitches.

God has eaten His own body.
Say farewell to the Big Cheese.

Brown Jenkin, Brown Jenkin, Brown Jenkin . . .
The universe echoes his name.

Amongst the Sargasso
(for W.H.H.)

Scott J. Couturier

The rank weed stretches endless,
coiling & clutching, fraught with foul
blossoms & pale crustaceans that crawl
over vine-draped hulks of ships long-belabored.

Bound from horizon to horizon by
masses of malign greenery that surge
& subside with the subtleties of each tide,
Sargasso hungry for derelicts to centennial abide:

& what amongst the weed thrives?
Colossal octopi ply those poisoned waters like
aqueous spiders, haunting a web of ghastly green—
malevolent eyes peer from depths unfathomed & fecund.

Tentacles scrape the deck clean—
prick the watchman from his post, vivisect
bleating sheep in their iron-bound pens. Around
the offal-port gather gargantuan crabs of mottled hue.

Their clicking! Like castanets of doom,
onyx eyes shimmering on slime-laved stalks.
A reek is in the wind—foul gust of the deep's decay,
harbinger for whatever abyssal horror will next besiege.

Now, a pale wreck looms from mists
that cling & coil about unshuttered lamps.
Something out-boils from her sea-rotted hold—
slick black hordes, legion eyes lurid amid brining damps.

The rank weed stretches endless:
becalmed & beset, bleak languid days
& nights of frighted huddling in berths reinforced
against the endless *scraping, scuttling, flopping, slopping.*

No escape or future to wistful crave,
nor fair sun, or breeze untainted by the weed's
awful fishy-vegetable fetor: no port towards which
to soulfully yearn. The Sargasso is prison, is home, is grave.

Notre Dame Is Burning!

Lori R. Lopez

Great shadows of wings expand against limestone.
There are times to defend, and moments to take flight.
Now it seems the latter as stiff bodies unfold, shaking feathers.
Rustling scales and fur. Odd shapes, horned heads arise.
"Leap to the balcony! Beware the smoke and heat!"

Not all of them, Gargoyles, Chimerae, have wings.
There are creatures of many ilk, at home in high places.
Some growl and pace or huddle in fear, watchful,
A hellish gleam reflected in the orbs of crouched monsters.
Far above the city, the river. Trapped on a stone fortress.

Notre Dame is burning! Unbelievable. Unbearable.
Cries of outrage echo across the Cathedral. A city wails—
A dreadful clash of sirens and bells. The world mourns—
An icon in jeopardy, charred and broken, sections crumbling.
Sacred objects must be spared, secrets and vows preserved.

"Strength, unity, courage!" shouts the snarlish horned ogre
At my side. Baboon-faced, humpbacked, he urges retreat to
Sky or land. Confined like many to climb, flee on foot, but
Where? Crowds gather below, weeping, praying. Some with
Eyeballs peeled. Can we slip unnoticed from lofty perches?

There are witnesses. Will they see? Might they wonder
If statues are missing? A number busy themselves at the base,

Rescuing relics, aiming streams of water, battling an inferno.
Will they save us? Will they care? Bizarre, grotesque in
Design. But we are part of the structure and beauty.

A few unruly goblins launch like sullen bats, brooding,
Abandoning belfries to wheel in protest. Gliding, veiled . . .
Obscured by plumes of gray yet risking detection, attention.
They screech with pain and horror, their haven in ruins,
Expressing for the flock a shared and shattered dismay.

Greedy tongues of fire lick at the night, voracious.
The unholy maelstrom roars, consuming the heart of our
Refuge, our castle. A mighty sanctuary from Monster-Slayers.
Long a bastion against Evil, invincible we believed.
Clinging to charred edges, avoiding the blaze, heads bow.

Will it stand no more? The pride of Paris, deconstructing—
Disintegrating, a noble centerpiece in flames, in peril,
Before granite gazes. The death of a grand lady, Notre Dame!
Citadel of lonely souls, gruesome specters, gloriously
Misshapen figures! A mother's ugly precious children . . .

Beloved, perched for ages, watching over streets, warning,
Guarding the gentle and forlorn, glaring down at the cruel,
Punishing the unjust. At times revered, feared. Repulsive yet
Cherished, almost angelic. "Come down!" summons a Chimera
Known as Stryga by humans, though he is no Vampire.

The hybrids flap to grip a balustrade and scowl, disturbed.
Seething orange flames smirch stone and iron. Wood melts to
Ash and embers. An orange-red glow lights darkness as Spire and
Rooftop burn. Cinders sail, borne on currents, the dance of
Warm and cold, an aerial Ballet; a grim concert without applause.

We must all adjust to change, as even mountains and cities
Erode. By nature I am just a bird. On Notre Dame I have
Roosted among Saints and Kings, myths and monsters. I have
Swooned to magnificent Organ songs, thrilled to the tunes of
Bells, the Rose Windows, the Buttresses jutting like a ribcage.

Carved by Mysticks, elite Stonemason-Masters; once a fierce
Line of defense, our numbers diminish—scarred by conflict.
Weathered, damaged, eventually retired. The small cadre of
Masters gone. They cannot repair us. None are left to
Separate truth from rumor, to realize the hazards.

She is vulnerable. A target of insidious trials, demonic or
Manmade. Our duty remains, to defeat sinister forces at work
Against the Lady, seeking to bring her down. Beleaguers . . .
They pose a constant threat. We can never rest, always
Vigilant. But this night we failed to prevent an attack.

"Who or what is responsible?" Emitting bass rumbles,
The Dragon settles behind in shade. "I will crack heads open,
Tear limbs, blacken bones!" An ape-like countenance blats,

Tongue protruding. Winged and horned, a Monkey-Beast
Charges to the Wyrm cloaked by fumes, hugging steep walls.

"Too late!" Vaulting, Stryga confronts the incensed Wyvern.
"Spare your hot breath for the next assault. It is in human hands
To save her now." Peering down in sorrow and despair.
"The Spire may collapse. The core is lost. We can merely
Hope like them. Who wishes to leave? I shall stay."

Voices reach them from every side. "I will stay!"
Only my neighbor the hunched Babewyn keeps silent,
Staring in dejection from his corner of the rail, like a statue.
"And you!" Stryga boldly steps toward him. "What are you,
A coward or sentinel?" I gasp in an ominous tone of quiet.

The last to respond utters a statement I will not forget:
"Mes amis, I share this post with all of you—and though
We were not born, we were crafted with affection, elaborate
Detail, every one unique, remarkable, yet possessed of common
Purpose and substance. In this we stand together, a family . . .

"Respect for the Past is as vital as optimism for the morrow.
We cannot desert Notre Dame in her hours of need any more
Than a man or a woman should abandon the mother who
Embraced and sheltered, guided and nurtured a child
To the best of her ability, out of the purest love . . .

"Let us combine our hopes. In her there is grace, history,
Art, inspiration, morals, compassion, fellowship at stake.
Reverence for symbols, for tradition has been shrugged off,
Discarded as insignificant in modern times like the sands
Of an hourglass. But each single grain is a treasure . . .

"Shining with virtue and value. Each moment we
Devote to this cause, protecting Our Lady of Paris,
Will be our deepest brightest honor. I stand with you,
My brethren, until the final block falls. However worn.
Gruff and faded. We marvelous beasts must hold on . . .

"To the end."

The Sweet Dreams of the Dead

James O'Melia

nestled in their niche of fast-approaching nothingness,
the remains of the dead stretch forth their thin hair
and their fungus-infested fingernails as long as they can
before they too fade away under the inhuman onslaught
of otherworldly organisms eating away at what was
while all the dank decaying corpses dream and
desperately try to keep it together;

despite appearances the dead do still dream,
though their images are no longer as vivid,
their memories continue yet to reside inside—
generating quick flashbacks of golden days that are done
and dear loved ones who carry on in the light
passing them by without a single thought
about this precious life that now counts for nought.

The Witch-Gallows

Josh Maybrook

In ages past, poor village maids accused
As witches hung upon it for their crime;
Now, high atop a hill, it stands unused,
The relic of a more barbaric time.
No flower ever seems to blossom near,
Nor ray of sunlight shine upon its beams;
For, thereabout, a sense of awful fear
Still lingers after centuries, it seems.
I saw it once in winter long ago,
When everything lay desolate and bare;
The sun had all but disappeared below
The frozen hills, and twilight filled the air;
And as a sickle moon began to rise,
I seemed to hear a din of ghostly cries.

Lord Death

Ashley Dioses

His icy glance invites the coldness in,
And yet just who am I to shy away?
He waits until I spill my every sin—
I swoon, his scented breath is sweet decay.
His skeletal embrace is what I crave,
His deathly kiss is candy I must taste.
His silk caress I've longed for in my grave;
I see him grin as I am laid to waste.

Our Lady of the Acherontia

Allan Rozinski

in the soft moonlight
her skin glows
like a luminous moth:
an angel in want of her lost wings

to find them might let her rise
in victory above this dying world

she raises her hands
in silent supplication
to the fearful who pass her by
seeming bound to a vow that forbids speech
though her very presence speaks
of waiting horrors and what they spell
more than if her lips could foretell

instead, you must rely on her eyes
to show you what they will:
black obsidian orbs, dark mirrors that hold
the reflection of your most torturous secrets
those you'd learned to hide from
in an uneasy truce
between the cruel weight of living
and the haunting echo
of death's siren call

* * *

all your sins, waiting to be revealed
lurking on the sinister border
restless demons you've kept
bound up and sealed away
now threatening to uncover
those dreaded memories
blooming wounds that never heal
in the recesses of your brain
growing wild in the rotting loam
the grotesque display
overwhelming everything
in a fertile frenzy of decay

if only we could will ourselves wings
to deliver us to a height
to aid in the search for a light to guide us
through this ocean of darkness
then to follow, sight absent sound,
and circle round what we believe
to be the holy heat of that fire
that draws us closer to the heart of our desire
so blinding, our vision might be lost
for daring to hope and dream

with the cost causing us to veer too close
to the flame that cares not that we seek it out
or that we burn alive
under the sustained white-hot gaze of that
indomitable eye

Legion

Benjamin Blake

I woke
Entangled in tree roots
In a forest, ancient and vast.

Now freed
I wandered a damp, narrow path
Through the monolithic trunks.
I saw her there
Walking just ahead.

I followed
A strange pain growing in my chest.
She was every girl I'd ever loved
And had left me
With blood on my hands.

And then she was gone
Leaving me standing
At the edge of a darkened abyss.
With nowhere else to go
I stepped in.

Where the New Gods Dwell

Maxwell I. Gold

When chemical thoughts again resurface in my mind, I'm reminded of a place where the new gods dwelled. Vast landscapes carved from dead planets whose cores of silver, gold, and iron covered Promethean forests of crystalline fauna with their remains. I longed to tread through the unmarked streets where forgotten civilizations lay in total ruin, while a towering dreadful homage to their ancient masters stood drenched in a hazy moonlight. Filled with rancor, I was embittered by those who once inhabited the awful elephantine cities of stone and blood. The savages couldn't understand the gods they worshipped.

Past the crumbling obelisks in my dreams, I walked toward jagged mountains that hung lazily over the city as if the Gods themselves were pressing them terribly against the horizon. Underneath, it felt as if they were preparing to end what remained of their experiment, swallowing my imagination, while some ardent chaos bowed in the presence of this malignancy beyond reason. Through the canyons of obsidian and eternity, I left all logic behind, as one shadow after another sliced past me as I approached an opening. Sensations that radiated through the night, a darkness that seemed bellow with a hunger older than time.

My neurons were completely sedated, unaware of the doom that collected upon them, like snow. Suddenly, standing right before me, towering into the spectral horizon, was a singular object, of which I cannot recall its proper name or any name for that matter, despite the banality of the thing that constricted my sight. It took everything I had to hold back the terror and every immeasurable sorrow that followed. The silver faces, gleaming with what appeared like diamond scales, smiling a most evil expression, whose molten images were forever seared into my heart. They laughed without sound, conveying silence that was even more chilling to bone and breath than the songs of sinister dreams bleeding inside my mind. I saw those empty black eyes, dying galaxies and bleeding hearts of yellow and orange stars whose own inevitable destruction pounded against my chest. They blinked, one after the other, waning and staring with their gaze affixed on me, and I was soon reminded of a place, of dank and metallic nightmares where they dwelled, and they had found me. They are coming, and soon, will be upon me.

   To those that may be so fortunate to read this, tread softly, for your dreams have cracks and the starquakes will break and shatter them as the Cyber Gods blink. For god's sake, do not blink.

Imaginary Friend

Ngo Binh Anh Khoa

His little girl had found a friend,
A funny guy, she said,
Whose portrait, drawn by her own hand,
Was placed upon her bed.

She did so since this friend had asked
To be allowed to stay
Forever in her heart and mind
Throughout each night and day.

But every time he asked to see
That picture she had made,
Refusals were what he received,
And she would not be swayed.

He left her thus with this new friend
Whom she'd met in a dream;
The girl did tend to make things up,
So normal it did seem.

Imaginary though it was,
This friend did lift her mood;
She'd talk more since her mother's death,
So everything was good.

But with each day that came and went,
She'd grow withdrawn and shy;
Few words would leave her paler lips,
And he did not know why.

Then, when her seventh birthday came,
She acted curiously
And softly spoke a desperate wish;
"Please leave me be," said she.

He yearned to find out what she meant
And so began to pry,
But she said naught, just looked at him,
And spoke a brief goodbye.

Her strange behavior added fuel
To his increasing dread;
No explanation, though, would come,
And to her room she fled.

That was the last time she was seen,
Whose muttered word rang true.
She'd disappeared from her locked room;
How it'd transpired, none knew.

Days turned to weeks, and weeks to months,
But not a trace was found;
The man's despair would further swell;
His mind in grief was drowned.

He'd latch onto each lead received
To keep the hope alive,
A flickering flame before a gale
With no chance to survive.

One night a sudden impulse came
And led him to her room.
The sight of all her things untouched
Intensified his gloom.

He grabbed her pillow without thought
And pressed it to his chest,
When from the pillowcase it fell,
A sheet of scribbled mess.

A sequence of most random shapes
Struck his bewildered gaze,
Which formed a spiral on the sheet,
A strange, hypnotic maze.

He, captivated, stared and stared,
But failed to comprehend
The meaning such weird symbols held,
And gave up in the end.

But when he turned the sheet around,
His heart was stabbed by fear;
A human-shaped thing came to view,
There grinning ear to ear.

Its upper face was dark beneath
The brim of its top hat;
The grin took up the lower half,
A horrid sight was that.

Serrated fangs from crimson gums
Were colored vividly
And so haphazardly arranged
On that monstrosity.

The man knew not how long he stared
At what his girl had drawn,
But when his wits at last returned,
It was already dawn.

The sunlight spreading on that page
Revealed a scrawly text
Beside his name and date of birth
In blood-red ink, "YOU'RE NEXT."

Lines on Austin Osman Spare's "Arbor Vitae"

Manuel Pérez-Campos

Under a crown of sunburnt leaves by turbid
stellar dust, the faint, translucently naked
spirit of tenuously elongated arms and great drooping
breasts leans halfway out of its maggot-splintered bole.
Grafted to a cliff's cramped oak through moon-drawn
spells by a coven jealous of her flair and hoodwink
craft, she fails once more the task of twisting free.
A lynx familiar crouches by tendered roots, its back
to her: its bondage nullified, it reacts not to that voice,
wanly resonant with lich-prone lusts, which has outslept
generations of villages. Exposed to fractures inside
crackled gale, her wizened boughs cumbered
by quirked runs of prismatic mould, she tends to dream
overmuch; and, out of spite, compels to fugue
or to lifelong gibber whoso rests in her shadow.

In the Forest, Where Wild Things Live

Claire Smith

He'd got in by the luck of wolves.
The cottage walls dotted
with photos of her granddaughter—
from newborn baby snaps
to prom night glory.

He padded into the parlour
after Grandma. A bowl of red apples
marked the middle of the table
    like a bull's-eye.

Lavender mixed with pee
crept up his nose.
Grandma in her nightdress
under a flannelette gown,
moccasins hiding her feet.

He saw bulging eyes,
swollen nostrils,
a silver moustache above her lips.

        *   *   *

As she spoke
a snarl escaped,
sickle-claws unsheathed,
steak-knife teeth broke free.

Still he was tempted by her promise:
After all, who would suffer
tough flesh of mutton
when you can revel in the succulence of lamb?

Melinoë

Wade German

"Dear child! How far, and through what impenetrable forests, have you been followed by the spectre of a werewolf? So long, to be haunted by terrible uncertainties! Let me soothe the ogre in your blood. You have run into my arms, thinking only to receive my care . . . Would I protect you? You see me as a mother, and so much is true. Are you an abortion, or merely real? I assure you, the werewolf cannot enter my home. But this is not my house; it belongs to him. I watched him build it from the bones of your ancestors, more than a thousand centuries ago. Feverish and pale, you struggle to peel off your face, which sucks to your head like a greedy cephalopod. Do you intend to carry on this way for eternity? Come, suckle at my breast, taste my black milk. It nurtures a breed of horses that may be seen only at night. Let me pretend that you do not wish to hear my sortilege: You shall harbour leeches in your womb. I am your true mother, but I have never borne a child."

Hell-Flower

Manuel Arenas

At Hecate's prompt, Hell-Flower blooms:
Ray florets open, awash instreams
Of moonshine splayed athwart crumbling tombs,
Dappling headstones in argent beams.

Bathing in full moon luminescence,
Wafting in fetor of Hell-mouth breath,
Perfumed airs of graveyard putrescence,
The potpourri of decaying death.

Drawing sustenance from coffined ground,
Fecund—yet foul—beyond potter's field,
Stretching its roots in unhallowed mound,
Cornucopia of unclean yield.

Puce petals frame a floral death's head,
Smiling with teeth absorbed from the soil.
Gnawing morsels purloined from the soil,
Wriggling amidst defiled charnel spoil.

Haunted

Ronald Terry

I've lived in the same place so long
I'm haunted by the residual shadow
of my younger self.
We speak to each other
quietly, without purpose.

I no longer remember my name,
free to be nothing seen or heard,
only touched by wind
breathing from the sun.

It spreads a relentless light
that never sleeps,
never lets the darkness rest,
never lets the night
dream itself awake.

He Who Waits

Frank Coffman

I am the Watcher, and I lie in wait
As long as Life has lasted on this Earth:
The hells of human tragedy, the heights of mirth,
The deeper happinesses, and the depths of hate.
All, all I've seen: the ends of Chance and Fate,
The years that bounty and the years that dearth
Have spun around this old Orb since its birth,
I've watched and waited here beside The Gate.

Oh yes, I have been waiting all these years,
Was ancient when Atlantis met its doom,
Watched Babel's Tower and great Pyramids grow.
I know the range of mankind's hopes and fears.
And know the thing most fear most is the tomb.
I wait. *Et in Arcadia Ego.*

Splenetic IV: After Baudelaire

Rahul Gupta

When the sky bears down, like the coverlid
sealing the maw of a sarcophagus,
in spiritual vivisepulture
of the cringing soul prey to acedia;
and the catafalque of the horizon
drapes us with days more dismal than the night;

when the globe suffocates like a dungeon
oubliette whose shadows are closing in
on Hope, that pipistrelle grazing her shrivelled
pinions on, and nuzzling at, the fœtid walls,
her leather webs a-skim the mildewed ceiling;

when the orgue of rain guillotines its grille
as portcullis to our vast prison-house,
and we feel the spider-legions weevilling
with venomed mandibles and spinnerets
to enfilade our skulls for nest and hive;

and across the parish, campaniles'
carillons at once go into spasm:
the tongue in every pealing gullet rolls,
haranguing with their tintinnabulations
God Himself with eardrum-splitting clangour,
as if extravagant and erring spectres
at matin hieing to their damned confine;

then the funeral cortege of hearses
observes, in sable crepe and muffled plumes,
my soul's salute of obsequy to Hope;
and then, despotic atrocity, ANGUISH,
implants her flag of conquest in my brain.

The Graves

Steven Withrow

I

When Conlan stepped within the square of stones,
Red leaves were tumbling in a sudden gust;
And the town's surveyor, trembling, thought there must
Be something to these do-not-enter zones.
His contract said to set up safety cones
And yellow tape around the land in trust;
But once inside he found that he could just
Stand dazed and close-to-blind in cold unknowns.

The map they gave him named the rock-walled site
As a former farmer's plat, or a cow's ground,
Yet grass alone now grew there, scarred with blight
As though crop circles compassed each stone mound
That marked a burial plot—the chill air bright
And loud (*so loud*)—or was it his pulse's pound?

II

Patrolman Wedge saw Conlan's empty car
Off-road at dawn, his quiet night shift done,
But didn't run the plates. In the fall sun
He knew at once who owned the Ford. At a bar
He liked, he'd met the guy—a football star
At Hollis High some years before—and none
Of his bells rang; he never touched his gun;
And yet the setting struck him as bizarre.

Wedge moved to search the car, then heard a crack
From in the yard. He called out to a wraith,
With no response. A queer thing held him back:
Where seven mounds were, now there was an eighth.
A white stone thrust from gummy earth, in truth,
The way his baby daughter cut a tooth.

A Conspiracy Penetrated

Carl E. Reed

A salute to Thomas Ligotti, Richard Dawkins, & Thomas Metzinger;
a sobering slap to the face of puppets.

Hearken, hubris: meat of moths!
You are not a thing of thought—
rather thought has fashioned thing:
a twitching puppet blind to strings
stretching eons back in time
to molecules a-stir in slime.

Self-conscious nothing, thou protests:
I opt & choose with every breath.
Exactly as the "thing machine"
expressed in regimenting genes,
jerks the puppet 'round & 'round
till death lays absurd puppet down.

Frozen Voices

Leigh Blackmore

The frozen voices sing a song of cold;
Deep lucent shadows steep the hillside bare—
Grim traceries upon the ancient mould
Where once there lay a palest gleam of gold.

Through soulless dusk, the freshets run so slow
'Neath crumbling bridges built in elder times.
The frozen voices rise, sing out their woe;
Insistent, clappered bells ring out their rhymes.

With hollow cheeks and eyes like dim, dark pools,
The deathless singers weary of their task.
Their litany proceeds; now these grim ghouls
Their frigid song continue like a masque,

With scanty hair and spindly limbs of ice.
The frozen singers' voices flare and fade.
In muted tones they tell the fatal price
They paid—their former lives they have betrayed.

Calling All Witches

Adele Gardner

We'll have a witches' bee,
swap lists of great Halloween books
and witch's brew recipes.
A witch in training knows
her best friend is her cat.
An independently minded witch
balances her checkbook before balancing her spells,
clips coupons and reads recipes first to determine
which ingredients she can afford to buy.
Witching is a calling: like poetry, it demands
determination, dedication, passion, and time—
and an independent income.
Better keep that full-time job.
Recipes for witchery can be found
by looking hard at crafts from your past—
from back in the day when being a witchwife
meant simple know-how and common sense
and home remedies and Women's Arts
like sewing and canny canning,
and an old wives' tale was the very best kind.
Look to the stitchery, the painstaking crochet patterns,
the crewelwork, the hems and seams lined up so perfectly
that corduroy weft and cotton print patterns match on both sides.
Check for your name sewed in the collar
and maybe a little charm or two,

like a sweet tiny bunny made of the same fabric as your front pocket
where it rides, peeking out of your dress:
"Just a little good luck to carry through your day"—
which maybe explains how you found your way safely home
when a careless bus driver
carried his lone remaining shy passenger
way out into the countryside
after her first day of school.

To the Wolves

Scott J. Couturier

A pale moon of gangrenous bale ascends;
wolves howl in homage to her lurid orb.
Over marshes by night my pathway wends;
November's snowfall each footfall absorbs.
Well know I the way, but—what can await
in that drear manse of my ancestral curse?
Torn portraiture, grave-mosses profligate
above each lintel, house carriage a hearse—
mercy, to be spared my homecoming date!
I waver as the pack draws nigh, bloodlust
resonant in each bleak, advancing bay.
I think of my father, once gone to dust:
foul magics I worked to revive his clay.

Now a gray slopping thing, master & lord:
I welcome the wolves with flick of my sword,
stomach slit & bowels eager out-poured.

Red Land, Black Pharaoh

Ann K. Schwader

No room for new gods here. Great Amun's rays
reach out in vain across the Western waste,
preserving no one. Trackless as the days
before Ptah spoke this planet, sands erased
our fragile scraps of history, replaced
all images save Set Kin-Slayer. Strange
& terrible, his temples half encased
in entropy, he claims us still. Yet change
creeps closer with each nightfall to arrange
our final visitation. Cloaked in flame
& prophecy, He offers in exchange
for all we are (or ever were) one name
out of his thousand. Lord of foredoomed lands,
Nyarlat waits. The wild beasts lick His hands.

Ouroboros

Frank Coffman

I

A symbol older than Egypt's eldritch land,
Where empty, towering tombs in ruin stand,
A Serpent circles, eating its own tail—
Has done so as the nations rise and fail,
Has done thus from the first. Eternity
Of how it was, how it is, how it shall be.
Greeks and Romans, Gnostics and Norse all knew
The "Tail Devourer" shows what's e'er been True:
The Cycles spin—no "widening gyre" to see.
The Circle always gains the victory.
Neither the wide nor narrow can prevail,
No matter how we strive to stop, assail
The spin. *The Alternation:* that's what's planned.
Those who accept this finally understand.

II

This larger vision of the snake is firm:
The ceaseless cycles of the Circled Wyrm.
Great *Jörmungandr* wraps around us all;
Of that "enormous magic" we're in thrall.

    Yet we who dwell within this "Mid-Earth's" coil—
Though living through small cycles, strife and toil,
Through pains, yet pleasures too, both joys and tears,
Pass through our time in a straight line of years!
The Greater Circles need not flaw nor foil
Our paths from birth to death, need not despoil
Each chance to answer to a Greater Call,
Do deeds worthy of Song—to Rise before we Fall.
Though now within this Dragon wild and wide . . .
    At last to go beyond and see Outside.

The Draining Chair

Thomas Tyrrell

All through my brother's christening
    I prayed that he would die.
He seemed a sickly scrawny child
    With a weak and reedy cry,

But he nuzzled at my mother's breast
    And grew fatter day by day.
The convent boat called at the dock
    And I was sent away.

While he was raised to power and wealth,
    The first-born son and heir,
I had been given to the Church
    To spend my life in prayer.

I had one friend and one alone;
    Her name was Isabel.
She stole me smiles and whispered words
    To cheer my lonely cell,
But prayer and penance wore her down
    And she became unwell.

I burnt sweet herbs and brought tisanes
    To ease her laboured breath.
I combed her hair and mopped her brow
    And closed her eyes in death.

For her I wept the tears I'd kept
    Dammed up the day I'd left
My parents' mansion; with her loss
    I truly was bereft.

The abbess called me to her side.
    In silence most profound
She took me through a hidden door
    And led me underground.

Stooping beneath a mouldering arch
    I reeled and shrieked aloud.
Dead Isabelle sat naked there
    Stripped even of her shroud!

"Kneel and pray," the abbess said,
    "Kneel and pray and know,
To this corruption at the last
    Your pampered flesh must go.

"However much we scheme and sin
    Or pray, weep and atone,
All that we come to in the end
    Is dust and rot and bone.

"Only the soul, intact and whole,
    Escapes this mortal prison
To be rejoined on Judgement Day
    Once Christ has re-arisen."

I bowed and knelt but could not pray.
    No holy thoughts arose
As week by week and day by day
    I watched her decompose.

Christ on his cross looked down at me
    Kindly, forgiving, wise.
Dead Isabelle looked down at me
    With maggots in her eyes.

Rich incense wafted to the roof,
    All while, clock-regular,
The putrefaction of her flesh
    Drip-dripped into a jar.

Nude skin will blush; hot blood will rush
    To flaming cheek and chin.
Nude bone displays to every gaze
    Its mirthless cynic grin.

And witnessing this hideous change
    From beauty to a clod
In wrath and grief and bitterness
    I cursed corruption's God.

Rising, I felt within my breast
    A gnawing pain and knew
My days of life were running out:
    Corruption had me too.

And now my lungs are choked with blood,
    My cheeks are clammy grey,
The worms of sin that writhe within
    Have wasted me away.

My fever-bed is tended by
    The abbess and her spies
Who watch me closely even though
    I can no longer rise,

Or else I'd creep up to the walls
    Before the matin bell,
And dare defy God's holy law
    Running the chance of Hell
To raise my eyes to the morning star
    And fall—as Lucifer fell.

* * *

O God, my God, be merciful,
    Hear a poor sinner's prayer!
Hide me in the unhallowed earth,
    Rapture me into air,
Don't let them take me to the vaults
    To rot upon a chair!

Retrieval

F. J. Bergmann

They tell us this planet is at an earlier stage, age
of frost accessible only by an arcane device. Ice
covers a critical artifact due to a cosmic blunder. Under
miles of snow, we approach science's border, order
robots to tunnel, see what they've brought. Ought
we disturb what's buried here, to melt and bleed? Lead
us to long-gone marvels: death is what we'll cheat. Heat
and light reveal horrible secrets, unveiled by cantrips (trips
into side passages are something they discourage). Rage
fills us: we've found what was sought—but won't send it. *End it.*

The Rider of the Pegasi

C. d. G. Nightingale

There was a being who spake with time,
Who rode unto vistas of sublime.
Whose eyes dared then to gleam the sun
And saddled the Pegasus on his run.

To distant lands from the fields we know,
How did thou collar time, and with which bow?
White Avian Feathers across the page,
Thou flew with spells the glow with age.

So do the Gods in mirth so high
Forget to birth prophets from the rye?
What harvest dreams doth thou now hum?
To awaken Mana-Yood from his drum.

I see now souls reincarnate,
Illuminate me toward that glittering gate.
For I've labored long in Elfland time,
The horns now blow ethereal rhyme.

Be thou my guide, O talisman of wonder,
Awaken from page and dreams asunder.
Through sleepy mists to fair Belzoond,
Watch the gods walk past the seven simoons.

These fancies I had not sought to see,
Till roused to the decks of Yann by Dunsany.
Now walking Bodrahans last light,
I've drunk from mirage water, so now to flight!

Testament of Doom: A Paean to Clark Ashton Smith

Manuel Pérez-Campos

Heralder, through lyre-trembled reverie, of
the coming of titanic amnesias: Hast thou
not soughed forth through deepmouthed
page the algid, vapory tentacles of Polarion
or out of erratic Achernar the cerulean flare-borne
petrifier plague? Lore of dissolutions attached
to an aleph amuses thee: Autodidact Machiavel
of phantom-vitiated, oriflammed Averoigne:
Kneller, through tales of medianic intrigue, of ennui:
True son of Tartarus thou art, whose necromantic
litanies fringe up-piled empires with uninterrupted
mist and mucilaginous darkness: Lo, thy
sublunary pageantry of overreachers ill-met
in fabled antenatal eras continues to breed
chimeras with one's thought long after thy black
tome, with its reckonings to deep time, is shut.

The Passive Vampire

Wade German

And comes the evening, when existence turns
Toward the wondrous glory of the dark.
The giant moon, ascendant in its arc,
Glows eerily, a green witch-lamp that burns
As all the colours of the darkness spread:
The shadows, in an alchemy of change,
Become in aspect wonderful and strange
Now being freed, like souls fled out the dead.

From sky to tree to mist-enshrouded ground,
Deep silence has assumed its lost domain.
Alive with sorceries and wisdom old,
Pale phantoms flourish in the dark unbound
As if in summons to some rite arcane . . .
And monstrous flowers, weird and black, unfold.

The Pores of Earth

Charles Lovecraft

> Great holes secretly are digged where earth's pores ought to suffice.
> —H. P. Lovecraft

The revelations came which blood could freeze,
And knees gave way. I had been fossicking
For something buried in deserted leas
Of earth, and found a trapdoor, moulding, sinking.
I nearly fainted at the prospect found,
Of dark forbidden secrets come to hand,
In isolated spot of ragged ground,
And pitched alone, of other folk abandoned.

I trembled as I raised the lid of fright,
But nothing found. The blackness curled, was void.
Slowly there seethed colossally to mind
A train of the bloodcurdling things of night.
A palsy gripped me, bristling, paranoid.
Arose a nasty rustling just behind.

Moribond

Manuel Arenas

All hail Moribond, Killer of Kings.
Grim, equitable ender of things.
None can escape his fast-felling grasp,
Once one's heartbeat he's sought to clasp.
Much less avoid the nigrescent haze,
Which swirls within his soul-quashing gaze.
Wanting for ears, he hears not the pleas,
As the ill-fated plead on their knees.
Their solicitations and direst cries
Rebound off his grin, haloed in flies.
Quailing in awe, they weep as they retch,
From the baneful balm swathing this fetch.
Viscera heaving in spurtive wrench,
Victims gasp at his bone-orchard stench.
His scythe rings like the dread Death Knell,
Cleaving the fey with impetus fell.
With a swipe of his osseous hands,
He gathers his prey in sable bands.
Then on his shoulders he deftly heaves
The souls he has stoked in mournful sheaves.

The Variant

Maxwell I. Gold

My mind had become nothing more than a malleable tissued plastic shell of cobwebbed shadows and muscled catacombs, haunted by cosmic ghouls and dreams of desolate oblivion. I don't know how long it had been since the inception by the Variant, but the screeching noises of text notifications, continual harbingers from snaps wrought by tweeting grotesquery and bytes of dust, flooded my senses.

Dead bits of consciousness, his hands over mine, and the whispers of what was and what could be collected like the bones of some ancient beast inside a forgotten tomb. To what end this decision was truly mine, I don't know, though, it seemed he knew my choices all too well. From how I liked my coffee, heavy with cream and sugar, to the precise and neurotic manner in the detail of how my clothes smelled. He really seemed to know everything. His trickery was apparent though, as he stood tall over the ruins of my fragmented body. My body? I'm not sure it was even mine anymore, or had he again seduced me with his miasmic words, stringing me along some wooded path with that alluring music of his.

The scent of aged laundry detergent, musty dreams, and a pile of rusted decision laid adjacent to my body without any hesitation, despite the mocking tones that floated to my ears. At least as far as I could understand them, or him, everything was too waxy. Malleable, remember? The room was spinning as I laid against him, rough and ample sized fingers clutching my shoulders with a desperate contingency of possessiveness and hunger. Falling, that's better. Deeper into a dank pit of insipid hopes and desire. I was struck suddenly with a paralyzing parenthesis; my limbs becoming as heavy as marble, reeking with an awful smell of cigarettes. Pins and needles stabbed at my neurons, slowly bleeding away while his laughter clogged my mind like some unholy sepsis. The foaming grey particulates of sleep gathered around my eyes like crusty foam, where I was unable to move or even blink from the immense weight of my own body, as if his paralysis had become stronger, more deadly. Transmutations and machinations, plastics and permeability; a Variant under the scar-tissue of his will, I'd become a puppet lying against him. Inhaling that intoxicating odor of his smoke-stained clothes, my mind had become nothing, but a malleable plastic.

To Gaelle Lacroix, Lone Survivor of the Trufort Massacre

Steven Withrow

You leave me sad and sleepless, and your story,
As much a folktale as a horror yarn,
A carnival of shades and sordid shames
From small Maine towns with long Acadian names,
Began at birth and ended with that gory
Sanguination in a storm-scarred barn.

You lost your mother and older sister then.
Your father, a long-haul trucker, was away
In a motel outside New York City when
The bloodshed started that November day,
A week before you made it, Gaelle, to five.
What kept you, after all you saw, alive?

The local paper branded it "mass murder,"
And called your mother's group a "Christian cult,"
Its leader, Jensen Carr, a "roving preacher"
And army vet from Kennebec. Consult
The next day's news: *Daughter of Preschool Teacher
Hides in Box Through Slayings; No One Heard Her–*

"Her" being *you*, of course—you stayed so silent
While Shepherd Carr and his "gun dogs" turned violent,
Shooting sixteen followers and, later,
Themselves, with Carr convinced there was a traitor
In his fold. But all (save you) were dead, and free
From needing to confess to treachery.

About those deaths, here's what you do not know:
Carr's target was a church in Orono
That had a lesbian woman as its pastor,
But when he sensed a snitch, the shepherd snapped
And, as you must recall, it all moved faster
Than anyone foresaw. It left you trapped

And shaking in an empty moving box.
Did your mother stash you there, or did you climb
Inside on instinct when the first shots sounded?
At four years old, did your sweetened sense of time
Go sour in you, like grapes to the fabled fox,
Or could you hear the cops had the barn surrounded?

Soon after, social services stepped in
And drove you to a safe house for the night
Where, hopefully, you slept, and slept, and woke
Only when your father came and spoke

To you in his most gentle voice. There might
Have been wolf-whiskers growing from his chin,

And you were in your crimson riding hood,
For you'd become at once a changeling child
That goblins gifted to a wifeless man.
How long until he drops you in the wood,
Abandons you to creatures of the wild?
You'd better run, as quickly as you can.

I'm pondering your French surname—*the cross*.
You're much too young to have its weight to bear.
The world has spared you, yet it fails to care.
I leave you to your nightmare and your loss.
I pray there'll be a lucky lightning-flash
To burn that old barn down to smoke and ash.

Dr. Ripper, I Presume?

Carl E. Reed

A top-hatted man of hot madness seeks
surcease of compulsion, respite in dreams
of crimson convulsions, echoing screams—
by fog-diffused gas light he strokes fair cheeks
then dagger-stabs heaving, fine-bosom'd physiques.
This gentleman of learning & leisure, esteemed
by patients & colleagues, is not what he seems.
In a steel-tabled basement he refines his techniques
upon medical cadavers but newly dead;
he kisses, caresses, anoints with rare oils
splayed temptress bodies—O succulence!—while
sordid bold visions limned hellfire red
through weird fevered brain, excited by toil
most foul, flame & flicker—moan-whisper—beguile.

Red Tresses

Scott C. Couturier

Your body to the ground: grace will caress
your quiet tomb, undress your bones of flesh,
tenderly & with care; your crimson tress
slick with blood, rain, & bitter tears enmeshed.
I will water stones for your memory—
nourish florets of mold with my weeping.
I, who yet live, but am nevermore free,
my heart interred too, in your cold keeping;
I wail your epitaph on night winds, pine
for even your corpse's touch. A red stain
spreads as feelers into my chambers vine,
hairs creeping from your grave into my vein.

So feed, my darling, by your mane of flame:
now darker dyed by gore—I gasp your name.

Classic Reprints

Strife

R. H. Barlow

The crimson blood-flecked orchid
Lifts its eyeless head, unsated from the feast
Of mangled flesh, and rears soft tentacles
Like wiry traps wherein to slay
The fair-haired man who nears its lair unknowing.
An hundred creepers, hairy-barbed,
Steal forth unto their prey; and rasp
His naked flesh. With scarce more terror than surprise
He strikes a double-bladed sword
Upon the clutching tentacles, and wounds
The red and noisome arm that spurts
Fresh blood upon his tunic. Nor is the creature
Vanquished, though its severed limbs
Lies awkwardly askew.
Again it clutches, brokenly, and finds
A grasp about its prey. The furry creepers
Twist and bind him while he strives
To hack the pulpy horror from its hold
And failing, tear with maddened haste
His sanguine body from the plant.
And as the dying man expires, blood
Both greenish-brown and human
Mingle on the ground.

[Previously unpublished. Written in April 1934.]

It Will Be Thus

Arthur Goodenough

It will be thus when I am dead:
The days will wax—the days will wane,
At eve the quiet stars will come
And look upon the world again.
And Night her ebon wings will spread
Upon the paths I may not tread.

It will be thus when I am dead:
The tides will ebb—the tides will flow,
The winds like messengers divine
Upon mysterious errands go.
And still its petals cast the rose
On many a grove where no one goes.

It will be thus when I am dead:
The meek will crouch before the strong;
The poor will clamour still for bread
And Truth give tribute to the wrong.
And Right will bleed as bleed it must,
Till God shall sanctify man's dust.

It will be thus when I am dead:
The days will walk in gold and grey;
The leaves will turn from brown to red
And by the wind be swept away.
But I shall spin no spider's web
Across the Great Abyss of Dread.

[First published in *Leaves* No. 1 (Summer 1937): 70.]

Reviews

The Sun Sings Loud and Clear

Donald Sidney-Fryer

LEAH BODINE DRAKE. *The Song of the Sun: Collected Writings.* Edited by David E. Schultz. Illustrations by Jason C. Eckhardt. New York: Hippocampus Press, 2020. 770 pp. $60.00 hc. ISBN 978-1-61498-266-1. $30.00 pb. ISBN 978-1-61498-267-8.

Let us announce at once that this book represents a magnificent achievement on the part of all who worked on it, directly or on its behalf. With such energy and strength and critical acumen as I still possess at eighty-four, let me proclaim and acclaim the physical fact of this volume or, I should say, tome. First, the poet herself, Leah Bodine Drake (1904–1964), even if long deceased. Second, the owner-editor of Hippocampus Press, Derrick Hussey, who has accomplished more than any other publisher we know (including August Derleth of Arkham House) to bring out quite a sizable library of collections by poets old and new. Third, David E. Schultz, the chief textual researcher, editor, bibliographer, and indexer, who put the volume together literally as an objective artifact, searching through the requisite libraries in the Midwest (Drake's own terrain). Fourth, the able and painstaking research coadjutor, Jordan Smith, who quested through the periodical resources of the New York Public Library to locate many published poems and other materials that might otherwise have lain unheralded and unknown. BRAVO, IF NOT BRAVISSIMO, TO THEM ALL!

  The big book itself, 6 × 9 × 1½, is the usual handsome item to which Hippocampus has accustomed us, the readers and connoisseurs of the house's publications. It is as complete a collected poems, plus miscellanea, as we could hope to have for long-term delectation and study. It has quite an able and substantial introduction full of biographical and bibliographical data put together by David E. Schultz. This is indeed an unparalleled collection of imaginative poetry (plus much else) comparable to the output of George Sterling and Clark Ashton Smith. This tome reveals a long life and career fulfilled, a major poet, especially a major woman poet, of which genus we can rarely have enough. Drake achieved wide publication during her lifetime both in the little magazines as well as in the fancier big-time ones. She won a good number of prestigious prizes, but had only two books of her own poetry published in her lifetime, the first, A *Hornbook for Witches* (Arkham House, 1950), now much sought by collectors, and at exorbitant prices.

Drake engaged in and sustained friendships with such remarkable authors as Manly Wade Wellman and C. S. Lewis, both of whom admired her poetry, but she had many other admirers as well. Early in her life and career she performed as a dancer and a model—yes, she was a handsome woman—and enjoyed her life and career very much, as well as the benefits accruing from her physical beauty. Lest we overlook it, we must mention here the striking cover (design by Dan Sauer), which incorporates an exotic drawing by Leah's mother, Cornelia B. Drake, depicting some beautiful Asian woman wearing an exotic Chinese-appearing robe, with a beloved peacock on a little swing in the upper left-hand corner. This art adds a lovely touch indeed!

In case we have not made it explicit enough, David E. Schultz in his usual role of typesetter for Hippocampus Press has beautifully laid out and typeset the entire tome. Jason C. Eckhardt as usual has provided some exceptional drawings, fifteen in all. We would assume that it is David who accomplished the section or subsection of alternate readings and unfinished poems. The introduction more than adequately details Drake's life and career. Because of her father's occupation of petroleum-seeker, her parents traveled around a great deal, finally settling down for an extended period in Evansville, Indiana (Schultz nicely supplies a little map on p. 27 to show the many cities where the family resided across the U.S.), where Leah primarily worked as a journalist, contributing an enormous amount of material to the *Evansville Courier*, reviewing among much else a staggering number of feature films from the major Hollywood studios. She complains about almost going blind from all the movies her job compelled her to witness and review.

She was married briefly, about a year, and then divorced; she did not care for married life, as appears obvious. She primarily lived with her parents as an adult and took care of them in their decline. She acted as a person of strong character and a certain distinct nobility. From her poetry and other materials Drake was evidently very well educated, well read, and intellectually sophisticated. But the interested reader can con all that in the introduction. There is evidently enough material still extant for a full-fledged biography, above all literary.

Just what exactly does this big book contain? Let us list the contents: the introduction, an extensive group of some fifty photographs, a list of drawings by Eckhardt, the collected poems (the largest section by far), alternate readings and unfinished poems, fiction (four short stories), nonfiction (a representative selection), published letters, unpublished letters, an appendix (of miscellanea by and about Drake), bibliography, indexes of titles and first lines of poems. The collected poems include the following sections or subsections: A Dream of Samarkand, Descent of Angels, Fantasy in a Forest, Honey from the Lion, Precarious Ground, We Move on Turning Stone, and The Face in the Water. The section titles derive from the titles of representative individual poems. What a wealth, what a plethora, what a treasure trove of wit, invention, whimsy, pure fantasy, and sheer imagination do we have here in this collection of collections! Even in those manifold poems presumably depicting the everyday or the commonplace, Drake retains an edge, an awareness of the Otherworldly, the Unseen, and the Other Side, constantly displays this extra sense as if it formed part of the five or six traditional senses, but somehow lying beyond them, as if within easy reach or summoning for those fortunate enough to invoke this outré sense through word, phrase, imagery, and pictorial or sculptural art.

Like Ashton Smith, Drake happened to live and practice her craft during what turned out to be a very barren period for traditional poetry and romanticism, from the 1920s through the 1960s, until the romantic renaissance that began with *The Lord of the Rings* by J. R. R. Tolkien and then Ballantine Books' Adult Fantasy Series under the editorial guidance of Lin Carter. (The Hollywood movies of the 1930s and 1940s furnish the one paramount exception to this dearth of serious romanticism in an intellectual or aesthetic sense.) Drake's own *Hornbook for Witches* appearing in 1950 stands at the virtual midpoint of those four or five barren decades.

Drake saw the beginning of the "big thaw" but Smith did not, even if he may have sensed that in a cyclic *manner* it was returning. In a way it forced such lone poetic exemplars back in upon themselves, and made what they still managed to create stronger and more vivid: Smith in the 1940s with his love poems inspired by Madelynne Greene, and Drake in the 1950s with her free-wheeling whimsy and somewhat gentler fantasy. They were less likely to compromise with the temper of a harsh and alien timescape. We can only be grateful that they persevered. Smith in the 1950s had at least the not inconsiderable comfort of a warm and loving wife and the home that she provided for him in an area—Monterey, Carmel, Pacific Grove—that he had first come to know at length during June 1912 under the aegis of his mentor, George Sterling. In consonance with that gentler time, let me quote some of Leah's lovely and unconventional lyrics, even if stemming from a somewhat later period. We quote the title poem "The Song of the Sun" from pp. 288-89; "Unlikely Story" from pp. 428-29; "To Certain Poetry Critics" from pp. 311-12; and last, marking a perfect poetic summit, "The Black Peacock" from p. 259.

Song of the Sun

Set in the streaming void
By the Hands that made the night,
The sun with a mighty voice
Shouts for his own delight.

With body and breath of fire,
Hung beyond hope or blame,
Nothing is his desire
But to roar with a living flame.

Ere the first planet spun
Tilt-wise around his throne
He sang the song of the sun
For the sake of the song alone.

An earth or two may bask
In his warmth—he does not care,
He is conscious of no task
Burdened upon him there.

And let who will employ
His powers for wrong or right:
He sings in his boundless joy
And the song of the sun is light.

And worlds may totter and fall
And all man's grief be done
Before the rapture fails
In the huge heart of the sun.

Unlikely Story

Down to the dragon's house of stone
The young knight came.
The dragon, sleeping on his throne,
Blazed like a flame

With coil on coil of body scaled
And pavonine,
Crested with gold and turquoise, mailed
With tourmaline.

And must he slay this bane of kings,—
This mosaic'd wonder,—
Robber of princesses,—whose wings
Were folded thunder?

A beast so perilous and bright
Gave earth a glory:
It seemed a counteract of right
To end its story.

More ancient than the mountained land
Or primal wood.
The great worm slept. With sword in hand
The young knight stood

Irresolute. The kings he knew
Were cruel, and all
The princesses were dull. He'd rue
Beyond recall

This deed! And yet he knew he had
High precedent . . . .
"The devil take tradition!" said
The knight, and went.

To Certain Poetry Critics

They say we shouldn't praise the violet
Purpling the secret hollows of the Spring,
Avoid the plough, the seasons ancient ring!
As for the moon—she mustn't rise or set
For any poet now! We must forget
Archaic words like beauty when we sing,
Deny the rose, and out to limbo fling
All that pre-dates the dynamo or jet!

But Nature still refuses to suppress
One ripening apple or one harvest-row
To please a critic! In a trite re-birth
Each year they come again, and men will bless
Hackneyed creation, and his songs will show
And love as old as Adam for the earth!

The Black Peacock

When the peaks of Kâf receive the dawn,
And the doe seeks water with her fawn,
Down in the gardens of the Khan
    Wakes the one black peacock.

An alien in the feathered herd
Of peacocks indigo and verde,
He is the sole obsidian bird,
    The proud black peacock.

In what strange jungle did he nest?
Beneath what peri's burning breast?—
This darkling prince shunned by the rest,—
    The lone black peacock?

Beside the marble-prisoned lakes
He cries his grief. His screaming wakes
The close, night-drenched acacia-brakes,
    The sad black peacock.

And humbler birds, grown silent there,
Thrill to the anger and despair
Of one too splendid and too rare:
    The proud lone sad black peacock.

    It is instructive and rather sobering to perceive Drake vis-à-vis Nora May French (1881–1907). Nora was born into the generation just before Leah's. She did not enjoy a fulfilled life as a person, nor a fulfilled career as a poet. Unhappy in love and life, she committed suicide at twenty-six, cutting everything short. Leah evidently did not need an ordinary romantic relationship in her life. She worked as a journalist, and in spite of difficulties (especially toward the end) she led a fulfilled life as a person and completed her career as a poet. This big book engineered for Hippocampus Press represents the vindication and fulfillment of Drake as a creative artist, even as *The Outer Gate* (Hippocampus Press, 2009) does the same for Nora May French, albeit in a much more limited compass. I have always felt a powerful affinity with Drake, even more so than with French. Following in the generation just after Drake's, I was born in 1934 but did not begin writing poetry seriously until much later. (I do not take into account here my earliest poems, my juvenilia, created when I was eleven and twelve during the winter of 1945–46, and then during that of 1946–47; these pieces amount to no more than ten poems.) I may note here some genuine resemblances between Drake and myself. Both Drake and I have written little fiction, that is, in prose. (Poetry, after all, is or can be a form of fiction.) Four of Drake's short stories exist. I have written a single novel and several prose-poems that could count as compact and concentrated short stories. (That does not rule out the possibility that I might not write fiction in the future.)

Drake as a journalist wrote an enormous amount of material in the form of reviews—concerts, all manner of books, literally thousands of movies. But she dedicated her real creative life to poetry. On the other hand, I as a freelance writer have written manifold essays mostly about books (poetry above all); some of these factor as reviews major and minor; this roughly connotes (but not in quantity) with the huge mass of Drake's journalistic writings. Like Drake, I have devoted much of my life to creating poetry, much of it in short forms with meter and rime, and a sizable amount of blank verse.

In my youth and adolescence during the latter 1930s and most of the 1940s and continuing on into the first half of the 1950s, thanks to both parents who worked in two different movie houses, I also witnessed thousands of movies produced by the leading Hollywood studios. Thus movies in the case of both poets may have honed our sense of the visual in their poetry, above all in regard to conscious imagery. In terms of the quantity of our poems it is a pure coincidence that, whereas Drake has written more than 360 pieces, I have composed some 370 pieces, or 380, counting juvenilia. Affinities can exist on many different levels among poets working in traditional forms, as this little accounting demonstrates, from Sterling and French and Smith to Drake and Sidney-Fryer. In this case the affinities are fairly tight and close-knit. Smith himself had become quite an admirer of Drake's work and acquired several copies of her first book of poems, the *Hornbook*.

A big sustained tide of applause for everyone involved: the original poet-journalist; the owner-editor of Hippocampus Press; the chief textual researcher-compiler-editor; and the painstaking research coadjutor: they have all come up with a huge and astonishing volume, and not to leave out the more than able artist responsible for the fifteen drawings (as listed on pp. 17–18). They have all done themselves proud in what they have achieved for dear and very gifted poet-painter-in-words: Leah Bodine Drake. No better homage to her memory could have come into existence than this compilation, the result of the assiduous labor by many conscientious persons. It stands as much a tribute to them as to the original poet-imagist. This tome remains as a sustained act of piety on behalf of a remarkable creative individual. As an elder poet I salute everyone who busied themselves in this pious and echt-protean enterprise. For me personally *The Song of the Sun* represents a crown jewel, or (rather) a jeweled crown, among the many recent productions by Hippocampus Press!

Terror and Poignancy

S. T. Joshi

STEVEN WITHROW. *The Bedlam Philharmonic & Other Poems*. n.p.: Lulu.com, 2020. 49 pp. $6.99 tpb.

This slim volume of poetry is remarkable in a number of ways. Steven Withrow—a veteran of *Spectral Realms*, as three of the poems in this book, including the title poem, have appeared in its pages—has evolved a distinctive poetic idiom that depends on the apparently paradoxical fusion of metrical precision and a relatively (and only superficially) mundane poetic idiom. The last page of this book provides the metrical forms of the various poems, and Withrow is not content with merely identifying a poem as a sonnet: he goes on to specify it as a "Pushkin sonnet" or an "Italian sonnet" or an "English sonnet." And yet, his language seems to reflect the "plain man's English" of such free-verse specialists as William Carlos Williams and Robert Lowell; it is as far from the elevated language of Clark Ashton Smith and his contemporary followers as it is from the deliberate obscurity of Eliot, Pound, and their congeners.

Consider the opening lines of "The Druggist's Curse":

> The druggist had been married twice. And once
> He'd finalized his second divorce and paid
> The settlement, he moved from Mapleshade
> (To stay in town, he'd have to be a dunce)
> Back east to Albany, where he's lived since.

This does not sound at all promising, if one is used to the idiom represented by "Bow down: I am the emperor of dreams." And yet, this poem proves insidiously effective in demonstrating how that seemingly innocuous druggist utilizes curses in a particularly nasty way.

There is, indeed, a danger in Withrow's method: largely eschewing the raw emotional thrust of a Sylvia Plath, he can at times fall into excessive austerity of feeling, and some of his poems don't have quite the pungent climax we might want. But his best poems—and there are many in this book—display a subtle but grim power that any weird poet would envy. "The Bedlam Philharmonic" is a notable example. I imagine the title is a play on "Berlin Philharmonic," especially under the direction of its legendary conductor, Herbert van Karajan. (The poem suggests a setting in Boston, but there is no Boston Philharmonic.) This poem—another instance of "musical horror," a genre that is suddenly flourishing in the work of Curtis M. Lawson and others—tells of a bored attendee of a concert who alone finds something anomalous, even horrifying, in some of the musicians. The poem builds to a climax in exactly the way a symphony does.

Much of Withrow's work deals with simple, even commonplace scenarios that are familiar to us all, and his brooding, stately verse brings out both their terror and their poignancy. "Interring Carter Jones" speaks keenly of the death of a child: "A pall is all he owns— / He who played with blocks / Now buried under stones." In "The Gray Kid," a boy calls a teen addiction hotline to say that he has taken a drug called Divine—and has seen God. This four-sonnet poem may suffer a bit of a letdown toward the end, but it movingly etches the wretched life that led that boy to addiction. In "To Gaelle Lacroix, Lone Survivor of the Trufort Massacre," a five-year-old girl is the sole survivor of a mass shooting in a family belonging to a fanatical Christian cult.

Other poems are of a somewhat more orthodox weirdness. In "The Green-Eyed Man," a painter is perplexed as to why she repeatedly depicts a man with green eyes on her canvases. The revelation leads to her self-destruction. Analogously, "This Borrowed Thing" tells of a woman who makes the ill-advised decision to wear her mother's wedding dress. Why ill-advised? Well, that mother had committed suicide, so we know that bad things will happen. The cheerless poem "Rats" grimly portrays the persistence and tenacity of this longtime foe of humanity.

We would like to see Withrow's next book to be a little more ample in scope and contents; but this small but potent booklet is a sufficient demonstration of the author's abundant abilities as a poet and storyteller. We look for even better things from him in the future.

A Queen of Dark Poetry

Sunni K Brock

CHRISTINA SNG. *A Collection of Dreamscapes.* n.p.: Raw Dog Screaming Press, 2020. 169 pp. $14.95 tpb.

A few years ago I had the pleasure of reviewing Christina Sng's poetry collection, *A Collection of Nightmares*, which I found delightful and game-changing for the genre. In this follow-up collection, she broadens her subject matter to the more fantastical, addressing fairy tales and mythical beings while still delivering beautiful unease with a style that keeps the reader engaged and entranced.

In this volume, she groups her selections thematically, but still retains a feeling of flow and connectedness throughout—as if you, as the reader, are dreaming along with her, transitioning easily from one vision to the next, guided by her masterful imagery. She achieves this through a feminine sensuality that envelops the full range of womanhood: light and dark, vulnerable and strong, deadly yet nurturing. She demonstrates this superbly in "The War of the Fall":

> And just like that,
> The battle was over.
> But a queen does not leave
> Her injured warriors
> On the battlefield,
>
> Not even when blood pours
> Out of her wounds like a river.

She tended to each fallen one
In place of their mothers,
Comforting the dying,

Thanking them
For their courage
Before she herself
Stumbled and paled
From her blood loss.

In the end, it is Ms. Sng who so deftly wields a royal penchant for creating her own worlds in which she shares her soul through her intense but delicate imagining of deeply held folklore. She has, in this collection, secured her throne as the reigning queen of dark fantastic poetry.

Notes on Contributors

Manuel Arenas currently resides in Phoenix, Arizona, where he writes his Gothic fantasies and dark ditties sheltered behind heavy curtains, as he shuns the oppressive orb that glares down on him from the cloudless, dust filled desert sky. His work has appeared in various genre publications, most notably in *Spectral Realms*.

Ross Balcom lives in Southern California. His poems have appeared in *Beyond Centauri, inkscrawl, Poetry Midwest, Scifaikuest, Star*Line*, and other publications. He is a frequent contributor to *Songs of Eretz Poetry Review*.

David Barker's latest books are *Witches in Dreamland*, a Lovecraftian novel written in collaboration with W. H. Pugmire, from Hippocampus Press, and *Half in Light, Half in Shadow*, a chapbook of weird short stories from Audient Void Publishing.

F. J. Bergmann edits poetry for *Mobius: The Journal of Social Change* and imagines tragedies on or near exoplanets. His work appears irregularly in *Analog, Asimov's, Polu Texni, Pulp Literature, Silver Blade*, and elsewhere. *A Catalogue of the Further Suns*, a collection of dystopian first-contact poems, won the 2017 Gold Line Press poetry chapbook contest and is available at fibitz.com.

Leigh Blackmore has written weird verse since age thirteen. He has lived in the Illawarra, New South Wales, Australia, for the last decade. He has edited *Terror Australis: Best Australian Horror* (1993) and *Midnight Echo 5* (2011) and written *Spores from Sharnoth & Other Madnesses* (2008). A nominee for SFPA's Rhysling Award (Best Long Poem), Leigh is also a four-time Ditmar Award nominee. He is currently assembling an edition of *The Selected Letters of Robert Bloch*.

Benjamin Blake was born in 1985 and grew up in the small town of Eltham, New Zealand. He is the author of the novel *The Devil's Children* and the poetry collections *Southpaw Nights, Standing on the Threshold of

Madness, *Dime Store Poetry*, and the forthcoming *Tenebrae in Aeternum*, to be published by Hippocampus Press.

Adam Bolivar, a native of Boston now residing in Portland, Oregon, has published his weird fiction and poetry in the pages of *Nameless*, the *Lovecraft eZine*, *Spectral Realms*, and Chaosium's *Steampunk Cthulhu* and *Atomic Age Cthulhu* anthologies. His latest collection, *The Lay of Old Hex*, was published in 2017 by Hippocampus Press.

Sunni K Brock's fiction and poetry combines science fiction, horror, fantasy, and erotica. As one-half of the team of JaSunni Productions, LLC and Cycatrix Press, she creates genre film and print with her husband, Jason.

Frank Coffman is a retired professor of college English, creative writing, and journalism. He has published speculative poetry, fiction, and scholarly essays in a variety of journals, magazines, and anthologies. His poetic magnum opus, *The Coven's Hornbook and Other Poems* (2019), has been followed by another large collection of speculative poetry, *Black Flames and Gleaming Shadows* (2020). Both books are available from Bold Venture Press and on Amazon.

Scott J. Couturier is a writer of the weird, grotesque, perverse, and darkly fantastic. His prose and poetry have appeared in numerous venues, including *The Audient Void*, *Spectral Realms*, *Hinnom Magazine*, *Eternal Haunted Summer*, *Weirdbook*, and the *Test Patterns & Pulps* series of anthologies from Planet X Publications. He lives an elusive reverie in the wilds of Northern Michigan.

Ashley Dioses is a writer of dark poetry and fiction from southern California. Her debut collection of dark traditional poetry, *Diary of a Sorceress*, was released in 2017 from Hippocampus Press.

Ian Futter began writing stories and poems in his childhood, but only lately has started to share them. One of his poems appears in *The Darke Phantastique* (Cycatrix Press, 2014), and he continues to produce dark fiction for admirers of the surreal.

Cataloging librarian **Adele Gardner** is an active member of HWA with a master's in English literature. She has published a poetry book (*Dreaming of Days in Astophel*) and more than 400 poems, stories, art, and essays in Flame Tree's *Lost Souls* and *Haunted House* anthologies, *Strange Horizons*, *NewMyths.com*, *Mythic Delirium*, *Horror Garage* (Paula Guran), and more. She recently curated the SFPA 2019 Halloween Poetry Reading (sfpoetry.com/halloween.html).

Wade German is the author of the poetry collections *The Ladies of the Everlasting Lichen and Other Relics* (Mount Abraxas Press, 2019) and *Dreams from a Black Nebula* (Hippocampus Press, 2014). In 2020, *Incantations/Sortilégios*, a selection of his verse in Portuguese translation, was published by Raphus Press and simultaneously released as a digital audio album.

Maxwell I. Gold is a Rhysling Award–nominated author of weird fiction, writing short stories and prose that center around his profane Cyber Gods Mythos. His work has appeared in numerous publications including *The Audient Void*, *Space and Time*, *Weirdbook*, and many others.

Rahul Gupta's poems, prose, and translations have appeared in *Agenda*, *Acumen*, *Equinox*, *Molly Bloom*, *British Intelligence*, *Wiðowinde*, and *The Society of Classical Poets*. His main enterprise is an Arthurian epic in "the most accomplished, imaginative, and technically-correct, alliterative verse since Tolkien" (Tom Shippey): two excerpts have been published hitherto, in *The Long Poem Magazine* and *The Temenos Academy Review*. Forthcoming work includes a volume of verse translations from Old English and Norse from Reaktion Books.

S. T. Joshi is a widely published critic and editor. He has prepared editions of the collected poetry of H. P. Lovecraft, Clark Ashton Smith, Donald Wandrei, George Sterling, and H. L. Mencken. He is the editor of *Spectral Realms*.

David C. Kopaska-Merkel assumed human form in the 1950s. As a cover, he edited *Star*line* in the late '90s and won the Rhysling award (long poem) in 2006 for "The Tin Men" (a collaboration with Kendall Evans). His poetry has been published in venues including *Asimov's*,

Strange Horizons, Polu Texni, Primate Cuisine, and *Night Cry.* He has written 31 books and edits *Dreams and Nightmares* magazine.

Lori R. Lopez is a quirky author, illustrator, poet, and songwriter who likes to wear hats. Her poetry collection *Darkverse: The Shadow Hours* was nominated for the 2018 Elgin Award, and two poems have been nominated for the 2020 Rhysling Award. Other titles include *The Dark Mister Snark, Leery Lane,* and *An Ill Wind Blows.* Learn about her books at fairyflyentertainment.com, a website shared with two talented sons.

Charles Lovecraft studies English at Macquarie University, Sydney. His main literary and life influences have been H. P. Lovecraft and macabre literature. More than 150 of his poems have been published. As publisher-editor he runs weird poetry imprint P'rea Press (www.preapress.com). He is currently working on a long Lovecraftian weird poem, *The Caller of Darkness,* and has edited thirty-four books.

Josh Maybrook is an American poet living in Edinburgh, Scotland. His poems, written largely in traditional verse forms, draw influence from weird fiction, classical mythology, and long walks in rural landscapes.

Ngo Binh Anh Khoa is a teacher of English in Ho Chi Minh City, Vietnam. In his free time, he enjoys daydreaming, reading, and occasionally writing poetry for personal entertainment. His speculative poems have appeared in NewMyths.com, *Heroic Fantasy Quarterly, The Audient Void,* and other venues.

C. de C. Nightingale is a short story writer, editor, and screenwriter currently living in Los Angeles. Born in Hong Kong in 1988, he spent his formative years in Southeast Asia before returning with his family to live and attend boarding school in the county of Cumbria, United Kingdom. He obtained his master's degree in creative writing in 2015 and has since been working for several weird and fantasy publications.

James O'Melia is a retired letter carrier who lives in Exton, Pennsylvania. His poems have appeared in *Procrastination, The Lynx,* and *Origins.* He is currently putting together his first collection of poetry.

K. A. Opperman is a poet with a predilection for the strange, the Gothic, and the grotesque, continuing the macabre and fantastical tradition of such luminaries as Poe, Clark Ashton Smith, and H. P. Lovecraft. His first verse collection, *The Crimson Tome,* was published by Hippocampus Press in 2015.

Manuel Pérez-Campos's poetry has appeared previously in *Spectral Realms* and *Weird Fiction Review*. A collection of his poetry in the key of the weird is in progress; so is a collection of ground-breaking essays on H. P. Lovecraft. He lives in Bayamón, Puerto Rico.

Andrey Pissantchev is a Bulgarian writer living in Leeds, UK, where he is hunkered down in expectation of the big, bitter end. He normally writes prose, and his stories have appeared in *Tall Tale TV, Weird and Whatnot,* and *Factor Four Magazine*. This is his first poetry publication.

Carl E. Reed is currently employed as the showroom manager for a window, siding, and door company just outside Chicago. Former jobs include U.S. marine, long-haul trucker, improvisational actor, cab driver, security guard, bus driver, door-to-door encyclopedia salesman, construction worker, and art show MC. His poetry has been published in the *Iconoclast* and *Spectral Realms*; short stories in *Black Gate* and *newWitch* magazines.

Allan Rozinski is a writer of speculative poetry and fiction. His poetry and fiction has most recently been accepted or published in *Spectral Realms, Weirdbook, Star*Line, The Literary Hatchet,* and *The 2020 Rhysling Anthology*. His 2020 Rhysling-nominated poems are "The Solace of the Father Moon" (short category) and "Cannibal Rex" (long category).

Ann K. Schwader lives and writes in Colorado. Her most recent collections are *Dark Energies* (P'rea Press, 2015) and *Twisted in Dream* (Hippocampus Press, 2011). A new collection, *Unquiet Stars,* is forthcoming from Weird House. Her *Wild Hunt of the Stars* (Sam's Dot, 2010) and *Dark Energies* were Bram Stoker Award finalists. In 2018, she received the Science Fiction & Fantasy Poetry Association's Grand Master award. She is also a two-time Rhysling Award winner.

Darrell Schweitzer is a short story writer and novelist, and former coeditor of *Weird Tales*. He has published much humorous Lovecraftian verse (*Non Compost Mentis* [Zadok Allen, 1993] et al.) and also has two serious poetry collections in print, *Groping toward the Light* (Wildside Press, 2000) and *Ghosts of Past and Future* (Wildside Press, 2008).

Donald Sidney-Fryer is the author of *Emperor of Dreams: A Clark Ashton Smith Bibliography* (Donald M. Grant, 1978), *The Atlantis Fragments* (Hippocampus Press, 2009), and many other volumes. He has edited Smith's *Poems in Prose* (Arkham House, 1965) and written many books and articles on California poets. His autobiography *Hobgoblin Apollo* (2016) and two volumes of miscellany, *Aesthetics Ho!* (2017) and *West of Wherevermore* (2019), have been published by Hippocampus Press.

Claire Smith writes poetry about other worlds. Her work regularly appears in *Spectral Realms*. Most recently her poems have also featured in *Songs of Eretz*, *Corvid Queen*, and *Illumen*. She holds an M.A. in English from the Open University and is currently studying for a Ph.D. in Literary and Critical Studies at the University of Gloucestershire. Claire lives in Gloucestershire, UK, with her husband and their very spoiled Tonkinese cat, Ishtar.

Oliver Smith is an artist and writer from Cheltenham, Gloucestershire, UK. His poetry has appeared in *Dreams & Nightmares*, *Eye to the Telescope*, *Illumen*, *Mirror Dance*, *Rivet*, *Spectral Realms*, *Star*Line*, and *Weirdbook*. His collection of stories, *Stars Beneath the Ships*, was published by Ex Occidente Press in 2017, and many of his previously anthologized stories and poems are collected in *Basilisk Soup and Other Fantasies*. Oliver is currently studying for a Ph.D. in Creative Writing.

Christina Sng is the Bram Stoker Award–winning author of *A Collection of Nightmares*, Elgin Award runner-up *Astropoetry*, and *A Collection of Dreamscapes*. Her poetry has received nominations in the Rhysling Awards and the Dwarf Stars, as well as honorable mentions in *The Year's Best Fantasy and Horror* and *The Best Horror of the Year*.

Tatiana Strange is a Gothic musician from Berlin. She is the author of *The Heroes of Dark Legends* and *Death Immortal*. In addition to her literary works she has also released a poetry EP on Bandcamp under the moniker Brazen Bloodshed, by which she is more commonly known.

Raised in Jackson and Meridian, Mississippi, **Ronald Terry** earned an M.A. in English from the University of Southern Mississippi, where he wrote his master's thesis on the poetry of Ted Hughes. For the past thirty years has worked as a technical writer in Dallas/Fort Worth, Texas. His poems have appeared in many print and online publications such as *Spectral Realms, Star*Line, Bete Noire, Poetrybay, Dead Snakes, Night Cry, Space and Time, Amanita Brandy, The Horror Zine, Eternal Haunted Summer*, among others.

Richard L. Tierney's *Collected Poems* appeared from Arkham House in 1981. A later volume of poetry was published as *Savage Menace and Other Poems of Horror* (P'rea Press, 2010). Tierney is also the author of *The Winds of Zarr* (Silver Scarab Press, 1975), *The House of the Toad* (Fedogan & Bremer, 1993), and many other works of horror and fantasy fiction.

Thomas Tyrrell lives in Birmingham, UK, where the Gothic is more Post-Industrial and less Southern. His short story "The Coronation Service" is published in *Hellfire Crossroads* 7, now available in paperback and Kindle, and his piratical poetry pamphlet, *The Poor Rogues Hang*, will be published by Mosaique Press in 2020. He has a Ph.D in English Literature from Cardiff University.

Mary Krawczak Wilson has written poetry, fiction, plays, articles, and essays. She was born in St. Paul, Minnesota, and moved to Seattle in 1991. Her most recent essay appeared in the *American Rationalist*.

Steven Withrow's most recent verse collection is *The Bedlam Philharmonic*. His poems appear in *Spectral Realms, Asimov's Science Fiction*, and *Dreams & Nightmares*. His short poem "The Sun Ships," from a collection of the same title, was nominated for a 2016 Rhysling Award from the Science Fiction & Fantasy Poetry Association. He lives in Falmouth, Massachusetts.

www.ingramcontent.com/pod-product-compliance
Lightning Source LLC
Chambersburg PA
CBHW060804050426
42449CB00008B/1523